Human Mechatronics:

The Double-Edged Power of Influence

By Craig Dubecki

Human Mechatronics™: The Double-Edged Power of Influence
Copyright © 2020 Craig Dubecki

ISBN: 978-1-988215-86-0

All rights reserved. No portion of this book may be reproduced mechanically, electronically, or by any other means, including photocopying, without permission of the publisher or author except in the case of brief quotations embodied in critical articles and reviews. It is illegal to copy this book, post it to a website, or distribute it by any other means without permission from the publisher or author.

Limits of Liability and Disclaimer of Warranty
The author and publisher shall not be liable for your misuse of the enclosed material. This book is strictly for informational and educational purposes only.

Warning – Disclaimer
The purpose of this book is to educate and entertain. The author and/or publisher do not guarantee that anyone following these techniques, suggestions, tips, ideas, or strategies will become successful. The author and/or publisher shall have neither liability nor responsibility to anyone with respect to any loss or damage caused, or alleged to be caused, directly or indirectly by the information contained in this book.

Layout and Design by
One Thousand Trees
www.onethousandtrees.com

Front and back covers created by Lisa Lawless (Lawless Creative).
Thanks to Elena Babkin for design influence.

Printed in Canada by
M&T Printing Group

Human Mechatronics™: The Double-Edged Power of Influence

Dedication	vii
Preface	xxi
Book 1: Part 1: Human Mechatronics™:	**1**
The Double-Edged Power of Influence	
Focus: A Look vs. A Glance	3
Chapter 1: Fight or Flight: A Brief History of Power and Survival	5
Chapter 2: Faith: The Stars, Religion, Politics	13
Chapter 3: Scotoma vs. Propaganda: Is It Your Mind or Someone Else's?	21
Chapter 4: Narcissism vs. Self-Esteem + Pride + Charisma	37
Chapter 5: The Power of Numbers: Mob & Herd Mentality	49
Chapter 6: Hate vs. Love: Why We Are Alive: Gratitude	63
Chapter 7: The World Order	69
Chapter 8: The Living Order™	73
Chapter 9: Me First! — When Things Work Out — Temptation — Fame	77
Chapter 10: The Speed Of Life Today	87
Chapter 11: Social Media Meltdown	91
Chapter 12: Are You Trapped?	99
About the Author	105
Suggested Further Readings	107

*Dedicated to those who seek
a world that is kind and fair,
with a commitment to social, racial, gender
and environmental justice.*

Human Mechatronics™: The Double-Edged Power of Influence

What is Power?

Human Mechatronics™: The Double-Edged Power of Influence

STOP!

Before you go any further,
think about that question.
Turn back the page and stare at the question.
Close your eyes, then answer it in your head.
When you feel you have a clear answer,
then carry on to the next page.

Human Mechatronics™: The Double-Edged Power of Influence

Do you feel POWER?

Have you lost your POWER?

Do you want POWER?

Human Mechatronics™: The Double-Edged Power of Influence

Do you want "TRUE" POWER?

I ask again... WHAT IS POWER?

Human Mechatronics™: The Double-Edged Power of Influence

On this planet we call Earth – our Home – we can all be found within the following double-edged list of personality/characteristic styles:

Happy people	Sad people
Content people	Frustrated people
Cheerful people	Angry people
Kind people	Mean people
People who lead by example	People who lead by control
People who lead by love	People who lead by hate
People challenging fear	People living in fear
People influenced by love	People influenced by hate
Generous people	Greedy people
Confident people	Narcissistic people
People who are team players	Self-centred people
Quiet people	Loud people
People who are fair	People who are biased
Shy people	Obnoxious people
Educated people	Ignorant people
Evolving people	Naïve people
Energetic people	Lazy people
People full of gratitude	People of entitlement
Open-minded people	Dogmatic people
People of peaceful resolve	People of confrontation
People who like themselves	People who fear themselves
People enjoy agreeable sex	Sexually abusing people
Conscientious people	Licentious people
People who are sincere	People who play games
Healthy people	Unhealthy people
Athletic people	Non-athletic people
Literate people	Non-literate people
People who will try	People who won't try
Satisfied people	Empty people
People of openness	People of bigotry
People of good self-esteem	People of low self-esteem
People supporting others	People who are bullies

Craig Dubecki

People who praise	People who ridicule
Constructive people	Destructive people
Creative people	Uncreative people
People who give	People who take
People of religion	People of their own faith
People of compassion	Bull-headed people
Spiritual people	Shallow people
Uplifting people	People who complain
Optimistic people	Pessimistic people
Anti-racist people	Racist people
Anti-xenophobic people	Xenophobic people
Opportunistic people	Altruistic people
Grateful people	Selfish people
People of harmony	People of chaos
People of decorum	People of debauchery
People who teach	People who judge
People who appreciate	People who ignore
People who help	People who turn and run
People who heal	People who infect
People defined by strength	People defined by weakness
Wise people	Blind people
People of comfort	Threatening people
Assertive people	Threatening people
Virtuous people	Unvirtuous people
People who are brave	People who are cowards
People who self-survive	People of privilege
People who try their best	People who are cockalorums
People of peace	People of war
Ethical people	Deceitful people
People of impartiality	People who live by jingoism
People who hug with arms	People who carry arms
Cool people	Not-so-cool people
People of all different skin colours	People of all different skin colours

Human Mechatronics™: The Double-Edged Power of Influence

The list could go on. There are also people who are mixtures of some, or even many, of these personality/characteristic types. There are good people, and there are bad people. I do not like labelling or even categorising people for it can cause social and cultural polarization; however, for the purpose of the two books, we must have some way to identify our distractions, or influence.

I do not intend to use this list to describe stereotypical archetypes; in other words, very typical examples of "a certain type of person." They may very well fit that way; however, I am using them to demonstrate how they may form as a leading "part" of one's personality, not as a whole.

Any and all of these people-types can carry a level of power, but what defines power in the first place? That is the question we must first answer.

Which side of the double-edged power of influence do you live by? Which edge have you been influenced by, or evolved from? You have the power to physically change only the present and the future. You do have the power to perceptually change the past; in other words, change, in your mind, how you view your past!

The last two questions I ask you before you read this book are, "How do you want to live as of right now?" and "How do you want to be remembered?"

That is what this book, and the second book, will help you figure out, if you wish, if you so desire.

Regardless, we all need, and should want to, find ways to live amongst each other. We must learn to coexist.

Preface

The word, Power, has been used in an endless number of phrases with a seemingly endless number of meanings.

I have heard, "knowledge is power." I have heard, "the power of the people," the "power of politics," the "power of free speech," "girl power," "money is power," "power nap," "power trip," "the power and the glory," and many, many more. I am not arguing any of these.

What I call "True Power" is not a perception, nor is it artificially created. It is an energy that lives within an individual. This is what I want to help you achieve for yourself. I'm only so altruistic. This is what I want to achieve for myself.

I hear many of you think, "Really? That's a very brash statement! Do you really think anyone can achieve this definition of 'True Power', Craig? And what is it?"

Then you ask me, using the powerful quote spoken by Detective "Dirty" Harry Callahan (Clint Eastwood in the 1973 movie, *Magnum Force*), "Well, do you feel power? Well do you, Craig?" Okay — not quite the exact quote but close ;-)

Funny you should ask because I ask myself this question a lot. It depends much on whether you view Power as a noun or a verb.

As a noun, Power becomes a status; a level achieved that many see themselves at. That is very subjective and, I believe, not measurable without bias. It easily leads to overly comparing one's "self", also known as individuality or ego, to others and determining/deciding that one is better than another. Sure, many times it is deserved achievement due to hard work.

However, if one views that higher status, especially with a title, as personal acceptance and distinction within a given hierarchy — that's when it can also become very judgmental. Humans never do that, judge one another, do they? Wink, wink...yeah, right! People do it all the time.

This power, as a noun, as a status, is perceived and craved by many. Oh, it carries weight and can move and influence the masses, but it is artificial. There probably was a lot of hard work involved; however; it is based on position or status compared to others.

Power as a verb is an action, a process, an understanding and thus a state of being, mindset or paradigm that one has with one's "self." That, I believe, is attainable and measurable.

But, and there are two "buts" here. The first is that as a verb, Power is intimately personal. It is not a subjective image we believe we portray to the world. It is an inner feeling of one's "self" that one feels and thus helps us believe in oneself. That's most important.

Secondly, when one feels it, one shows it, and through that positive energy — other people then see it and in turn feed their positive energy to others! That can be good! Of course people feed off of each other — both ways: positive and negative energy. The trick is not to live one's life negatively based on the response of others. When we feel that control over how we handle life, it, and I mean the feeling of Power — all starts here. This is where we start to rock!

As a verb, then yes — I have achieved true "Power," but not as a constant. It will never be a constant without my own oversight — checks and balances, over how I am thinking. That is part of being human versus being a robot. The human mind fluctuates, and thus so do my actions.

Like the list at the beginning of the book, power, and thus influence, comes with a double-edge: one side of power can be constructive; one side of power can be destructive.

Just so we are not misdirected, this Power I am talking about here is the most intense, rewarding, inspiring, attractive and intoxicatingly sustained feeling a human being can ever have (yes, my opinion).

This Power is the drive, the catalyst, the passion that is behind everything we strive for in our lives.

This Power is what will make you happy regardless of whatever else is going on in your life. It will keep you alive when the world tries its best to bring us down from any positive principles or feelings we have, which it does with brutal and painful force.

This Power is something I'm sure your parents, teachers, coaches, employers, maybe even your partners and, yes, most of all yourself, have told you to do.

Regardless of race, sex, education, age or financial situation, many people in this world might be confused by thinking Power is one of the following:

- Control in any way over another human being, or group of human beings, or any living creature.
- Intimidation thrust upon another living being:
  - As a parent who is supposed to guide the acquiring of a child's aptitude so the child can lead a life of positive purpose within the living and world order.
  - A teacher for the very same reasons
  - As a leader of a group, team, nation, religion, culture or government.
  - As a driver of a vehicle, such as is the case with tailgating, road rage and even the design of a vehicle (I refuse to believe that the carmaker Audi did not know the latest design of headlights would be of an angry expression when the lights are on at night).
  - Any person in a position of leadership/authority who abuses the power of position bestowed to them.

- Anyone cowering cowardly behind "freedom of speech" as an excuse for advocating hatred and/or hurt.
- A person who covets nepotism and through that privilege, believes one is omnipotent, and therefore lives a life of entitlement.
- Any person who, through their own advancement, refuses to be grateful and remain humble, but instead uses their blessed position in a self-serving way through intimidation and manipulation, and in order to counter their own low self-esteem, degrades and puts others down. If you don't retain the ability to be humble and grateful, this can easily lead to feeling an omnipotent and arrogant misguided power.
- Sometimes one attempts to create their own perceived power by being louder than all others in order to control the atmosphere and/or narrative.

More on this later when we talk about narcissism.

For those of you who live and believe that any of these aforementioned perceptions of power are true, I will tell you right now — you are sadly misguided! It may seem powerful on the surface, but it is only temporary and has no strength to it. It becomes a popularity contest ready to shift in an instant.

This kind of power comes from a need to boost one's own self-esteem — one's own feelings about oneself. By belittling, intimidating, and controlling others - the desire is to make others feel weak in order to make one feel good. Based on insecurities and possibly even hatred of who you are when compared to others, it all comes down to how one feels about oneself in comparison to others.

In a scene from the 1993 movie *Tombstone*, when Val Kilmer is sick in bed and Kurt Russell is standing looking at him, Val talks about the murderous villain, Johnny Ringo.

Kurt: What makes a man like Ringo, Doc, makes him do the things he does?
Val: A man like Ringo had a great empty hole right through the middle of him. He can never kill enough or, steal enough, or inflict enough pain to ever fill it.
Kurt: What does he need?
Val: Revenge
Kurt: For what?
Val: Being born.

Sadly, there are too many people that feel this anger and sadness, for real. What a paradox that must be; to try and live amongst the living yet feel dead inside! Why is that? Stay tuned.

Let's have a little bit of fun. It's time to acknowledge who we are before we tackle how we are distracted/influenced and, how to focus through all that influence.

It may feel uncomfortable at first, but take this book, go stand in front of a mirror, look at yourself, smile, and based on what you've read so far, ask the following questions:

1st question: Who am I?

Tough question? Have fun describing "you." Pause if you wish, then answer the question. Now answer it again out loud. If you feel super-courageous, even write all your answers down. Keep smiling.

2nd question: What influences helped make me who I am?

Pause if you wish, then answer the question. Now answer it again out loud.

3rd question: Did I decide, of my own free will, to be who I am today?

Pause if you wish, then answer the question. Now answer it again out loud.

4th question (bonus): Am I honestly happy with who and where I am today?

Craig Dubecki

Pause if you wish, then answer the question. Now answer it again out loud. Keep smiling.

Now let's see if any of that changes after you read the remainder of this book.

Human Mechatronics™: The Double-Edged Power of Influence

TRUE POWER?

FOCUS!

The True Power I am talking about
is the ability to:
FOCUS

Focus =
Concentration

Focus =
In charge of our own mind

Focus =
Owning one's "Self"

Focus =
Handling distractions
while staying on target

Focus =
Achieving quicker redirection to the positive
when negative thoughts surface!

Focus = True Power!

Introduction

To clarify, this kind of Focus has nothing to do with vision strength. It has nothing to do with wearing corrective lenses of any type. A person could be blind and still be able to master the level of focusing illustrated in this book. Open your mind, stay patient, and keep reading.

This Power called Focus is something maybe even you have told yourself to do. Yes you have! And, you likely thought you were doing it — focusing, but...

Did you really understand what you were doing ... or how, or why?

I have spent easily the better part of my life, somewhere near forty years, struggling to understand and find sustained focus. There were/are many reasons behind that struggle. Many of them are explained in my first book, *So, You Just Want To Be A Rock Star*. The remainder of them, along with the science behind that struggle, will be explained here.

Why Focus? What makes the ability to Focus the true Power? Let me ask you a question. Do you like feeling sad? Let me ask you a different question. Do you like feeling overwhelmed? How about feeling confused? Do you like feeling helpless? Do you like feeling you are without purpose — without direction, out of place? Do you like feeling powerless when it comes to controlling some part of your life? Forget about grouping all of these together; I bet you don't like feeling any one of these! How about this one: do you feel like you have lived too much under the influence of others? Hang on to this idea of influence.

I have felt all of the above! At one time or another, these have all consumed me — sometimes one at a time, sometimes grouped into a huge mess of shit hitting the fan. They no longer do!! Oh, they still come, trying their best to take control. Now, however, I am able to catch them before they pass through my conscious mind and consume the vibrations of my subconscious machine —my human machine —my "self"!

Today's society is subjected to a very sophisticated, psychologically and marketed news media and social media onslaught. Sure, it's nice to be reminded … "think positive," "It's up to you," "Don't look back," "Akuna Metada" (from the movie, *The Lion King*), "Vote for me!" and so on. Social media is inundated with 1-page slides repetitively relaying one-liners as subliminal pick-me-ups (more on this in the chapter: Social Media Meltdown).

The problem is our thoughts are not a light switch. Yes, constant reminders and news help change them suddenly for a minute, hour, maybe a day, even a week. However, if we don't understand the root cause, and we don't understand how to control our thoughts, we revert back to the *Star Wars* Dark Side, sometimes with vengeance if we are filled with anger — especially about ourselves. And don't fool yourself. That anger may be directed at someone else but the only reason the anger surfaced is because of how you, maybe even in just that moment, feel deep down about your "self," aka, your own self-esteem (your self-worth or ego).

So, how can we prevent that? How can we keep positive about our "self"?

Why did you choose this book series? I will let you answer that for yourself. In fact, write it down, right now! By choosing a book with this title, where do you think you are headed? What will you gain?

When you have finished the final chapter, compare how you feel at that very moment to how you felt this very moment when you wrote your expectation down.

These books introduce the following studies: Human Mechatronics™, DotsDoConnect™, Quadrantic Cognition™, and The WYLIWYG® Principle — pronounced, "will-ee-wig." WYLIWYG: Where You Look Is Where You Go®.

These terms are all new spins to human thought- processing, or CB (Cognitive Behaviour). WYLIWYG® is an acronym, a term, used by driving instructors. Don't laugh —you have no idea!! (Explained in Part 4).

You don't hear any of these terms talked about much —if at all. After today, you will. I hope they help and become tattoos on your mind — common objects, like when you buy a vehicle that you can't remember ever seeing on the road. To some of us, this is a big thing: owning something (vehicle) that we feel is unique. That makes us feel special. Yes it does, if only to our self! However, once we start driving that new vehicle, we start to see all the other identical vehicles that are on the road —just maybe different colours. Where'd they come from? They were always there. It's just that our mind was not trained to acknowledge and recognize them because we didn't have to; we had no interest.

If you want to better your life, learn about these new terms with as much of an open mind as you can muster, and YOU WILL better your life.

Oh, but you say you are already bettering your life. You are reading all kinds of personal growth books; books by Napoleon Hill, Maxwell Maltz, Don Miguel Ruiz, Rhonda Byrne, Eckhart Tolle, etc... Good for you! Oh, and you are saying you have studied Tony Robbins, Esther Hicks, Plato, Socrates, Sigmund

Freud, Carl Yung and Alfred Adler, and that you have spent $5,000 on a Bob Proctor or Dale Carnegie course designed to help you change your paradigm and be a better salesperson in order to discover your archetype and get rich. Excellent! Maybe you are on the right track for you.

But, if you cannot Focus the way you need to, if you do not understand how to control distractions, you will be spinning your own wheels and not absorbing all this great material the way you want to — and paid for.

When I was a kid, I heard so often from my educators that, "Craig, you have true leadership skills! All you need to do is focus better! Craig, when you start to focus, you will start to reach your potential!" Everyone was telling me I had great abilities but I needed to Focus.

No one back then, none of these aforementioned world-class motivators and personal growth gurus, not even Tony Robbins himself, who I saw live from the twelfth row, performing for 4½ hours with 9,000 other people in Toronto, Canada, taught me what Focus "IS"!!!! They all told me to do it, but what the hell is it?

So, that is what I am doing with these books and new studies/science.

Does any of this sound familiar? I have done it all, having spent decades gathering up information, getting educated, all to understand how we humans work —how our minds work and why we do what we do. I am not a scientist. I do not have a PhD in anything. I have university credits and a college diploma. I have been a teacher —a "professor" of driving motor vehicles. Yes, you read right, I have been a driving instructor —one of the most underappreciated professions that I know of. I was a supervisor with Young Drivers of Canada (YD), and I taught people to become driving instructors. More than most anyone else, I helped massive amounts of people, physically and mentally, learn how to stay alive in road trenches, and to defend themselves while using a weapon of mass destruction (motorized vehicle) when in the wrong hands or the wrong minds.

YD is one of, if not the best and most comprehensive driving school anywhere. We did not just teach driving a motor vehicle; we taught how to be aware, focus, spot the problems, and stay alive on the road which, transcended into day-to-day life. As an instructor, it was like playing a game of chess — I had learned to be five or more steps ahead from what I knew my driver was thinking. What do you think teaching all that takes, as far as a person's character is concerned?   Just let that sink in for a moment.

Earlier I said about the mind fluctuating — "That is part of being human versus being a robot." With this book title, get rid of the word, "Human," and you are left with "Mechatronics." Mechatronics is the wave of the future. Some of the most prestigious universities in the world teach specialized courses on Mechatronics. Yet the world seems completely naive to Human Mechatronics™.

To quote the company, Brose (www.brose.com) and their specialty in manufacturing for the automotive and consumer products amongst many other industries:
Mechatronics is the combination of different fields of engineering to design and control mechanisms that move.
At the core, Mechatronics is the combination of mechanical engineering to make a robust physical part, electrical engineering to design circuits that operate in the required environment, and software engineering to write code to control the combined system in its environment.
Electronics and mechanics integrate to make up the partnership that is known as Mechatronics.

Human Mechatronics™, therefore, is our own Human Machine. It was mechanically engineered and created (by someone we all have faith in) as a robust physical part. It was electrically engineered and created (still, by someone we only have faith in) to connect the circuitry amongst all the various systems that must work in unison within our robust physical machine. It comes with a brain, which works as our mind. It can be changed in endless ways through that Software Engineering part of Mechatronics. It's ready, no, it WANTS to be programmed and be able to give everything our Human Machine wants to do.

In order to learn how to focus at an extreme level, you have to understand, somewhat, how the human machine and, in particular, the human mind works, and how thinking has evolved over the years and centuries. In this two-book series, *Human Mechatronics™: The Double-Edged Power of Influence* and, *Human Mechatronics™: The Power of Focus Introducing The WYLIWYG® Principle,* I will review and define in layperson's terms, in other words, in non-scientific or non-sesquipedalian (numerous syllables as in medical/legal style), how the brain and mind work and how and why our thinking is influenced.

Quadrantic Cognition™ deals with how much distraction and focus the mind can actually handle and accomplish in a given moment. It is paramount to controlling what is passing through our mind and into our personal vibration state.

DotsDoConnect™ is an understanding we need in order to deal with distractions of the past and focus on where we want to go. It helps bring peace to our past. Is that something you would like to achieve for yourself?

Then, and only then, will you be able to process and embrace The WYLIWYG® Principle. Then, you learn the science of laser focusing. WYLIWYG: Where You Look Is Where You Go®, is so important to me that I have registered it, and the other three terms, as official trademarks. You will find that it's something you have known about all your life — right from when you were a baby.

Human Mechatronics™: The Double-Edged Power of Influence

First, however, we must have a firm understanding of the power behind influence. Without this understanding, evolving for the better will remain much more a challenge than it should be.

So, now for the real kicker — this is all being released in two books. I had hoped for, and worked so hard, to put it all in one; however, I am also human.

My focus and tenacity has been the best I could give. Due to these unprecedented times we are in, with the Covid19 virus and polarization of nations happening before our eyes, I felt I needed to release Part 1 now. Part 2, 3, and 4 should be released in the fall of 2020.

(I am typing this on May 30, 2020, while the United States and much more of the world is in pain due to the death, under police control in Minneapolis, Minnesota, of 46 year-old black American, George Floyd.) I hold no secrets.

Both books reference historical events, music and lyrics, define terms through the dictionary, and draw parallels to movies (*Star Wars, Dark Side, Magnum Force*, and the lines from the movie *Tombstone*, to name a few).

This book in particular, uses the mental skills of many familiar activities such as sports, being a pedestrian, and driving a vehicle or even a bicycle, to define principles and thought behaviour (cognition).

I will share my opinions only to encourage you to open up and expand your mind and beliefs. My hope is that if your life has evolved to where you are today based on negative influences - ones that have caused you to lose your "self" and live more on the dark side of life, you will start to realize the powers that you actually have within yourself to change for the good of you, and for the good of a humanistic world.

I am not here to teach. I share all this with you hoping that you will learn new tools to help you evolve further into who you are, or into the person you envision.

Craig Dubecki

If you want to have the ability to make the best out of your life, it all starts here! True Power is achieved through True Focus.

There ya go! I hope you enjoy reading this book. Thank you for the investment you have made in yourself by doing so.

Part 1
Human Mechatronics™

The Double-Edged Power
Of Influence

Focus: A Look versus a Glance

When you ride a bicycle or drive a car, you learn to look well ahead in order to stay straight and upright. You need to then learn to move your eyes to spot the problems. If you don't, you could be killed, or kill someone; but if you look at a problem, you will no longer stay straight and possibly kill someone yourself. What you look at becomes your influence.

Therefore, *you learn to look well* ahead but every two seconds *move your eyes* and *glance* at a problem, then you immediately *look well ahead* again. But then you can *glance* at the same, or another, problem again — then *look well ahead*. Get the pattern? You can keep doing this to stay on the road, in your path, yet deal with a problem.

A *glance* is *no more than a one-second look-away (at the most). One second — that is all*. Do this as much as you need to, but you quickly go back to *looking well ahead* — to your target.

I'm going to repeat all this but change one or two words along the way.

When you travel through life, when you *drive towards your goals*, you learn to *look well ahead* in order to stay straight and focused. You need to then learn to *move your eyes* to deal with distractions. If you look at a distraction, you will no longer stay straight and focused. Therefore, you learn to *look well ahead* every single day but *move your eyes* and *glance at a problem, or distraction*. Then, you immediately *look well ahead* again — to where you want to go in life. *Glance* at the distraction — then *look well ahead*. Get the pattern?

This is all controlled by the mind. Your eyes do not move unless your mind tells them to. Consciously force yourself to get into a routine of moving your eyes as such. Then your mind starts to acknowledge this new pattern as its new routine.

Which is the chicken and which is the egg, you ask? Which comes first: the forcing oneself or the mind acknowledging the action? In reality, it is all the same. It is all about your mind.

You have used your mind to try a new idea, and you have allowed your mind to accept it. That is a decision you consciously have made. It is the same tool used, but there is a difference in the process. I will explain this in Part 4 when we dive into the art of focusing with The WYLIWYG® Principle. Learn this first to stay focused on the road, in your path towards your goal, yet deal with a problem.

I can't state this enough; when operating a moving bicycle or motor vehicle, a Glance is no more than a one-second look-away. This will help you stay alive. One second — that is all. Remember, it's your mind that tells your eyes to move. Do this as much as you need to but quickly go back to *looking well ahead*. This is what you need to learn to do in living your own life. Where do you want to go in your life?

What Are You Looking At?

Chapter 1

Fight or Flight:
A Brief History of Fear, Survival & Power

In High School I never cared for history. To me, being a hormonally driven, athletic teenager, history was very boring. Big mistake! I was so naïve. History is now fascinating to me. It helps me, as you will find out in later chapters, "Connect The Dots." I love history for how it teaches how and why things were done in the past, and explains the phases the Earth, humanity, and the human body itself, have evolved through.

Regardless of culture or geography, once humans appeared, people through the ages have had one thing in common: the makeup of their own Human Machine.

With all the technology, with all the computerized modelling, do you think we, in these times of 2020 and beyond, are so special when compared to people of the past? Do you think we are so much better, smarter and gifted because of our "advanced" technology and science?

I believe we are. I believe we at least have the opportunity to be so. I also believe that misuse of it all can now be far more damaging than ever before.

From the very beginning of humankind — whether you believe in the primeval history of Adam and Eve, or Darwin's theory of evolution with apes becoming cavemen then eventually becoming modern day "us" — when the first two of any species met they likely felt, in this order: surprise, curiosity, and then fear. The decision was then, "fight or flight." This expression will be explained more in Part 2, which focuses on the mind and how the limbic system, in particular the hypothalamus, works — but essentially it's how we deal with a surprise.

To find true and sustainable Focus, one must understand how the mind works. In this first meeting of species, their decision was sheer reaction. There would be no defined response as response is built upon wisdom, which in turn is built upon experiences and neurological coding. There would have been no discussion. Adam would not have been a gentleman, extending out his hand to Eve saying, "Hello, my name is Adam. It's so nice to meet you!" The two cavemen, or even the apes, would not have clinched their fists and gently knocked them together saying, "Hey Bro, nice to meet you." There would have been no verbal communication as there was no language yet. At least there has never been proof of language — only theories.

Think about this — what would even be going through their minds? Language to that moment of first encounter had not yet been created; therefore, what "could" possibly have been going through their minds? Nothing, that's what! They could not hesitate and recognize, define and analyse what they saw and "think" about it because they could not yet think. That's what we do now, but not back then. In the beginning it was a pure reaction based on how the mind was created to work for us – to protect us – to help us survive.

Science is finally discovering this about the brain. This is still part of that "missing link" of human evolution as there is no proof — no proof at all. All writings and beliefs are exactly that: beliefs. They are theories based on personal and maybe even scientific assumption, many of which are supported by rhetoric and conjecture, but they are not fact!

However, in these good ol' high-tech days, even though most of us feel that we are masters at *recognizing, defining, analyzing* and *measuring* anything when we see it, the response of how we *improve, standardize* and *implement* is not always for the best. And yes, those seven actions I just listed are also the main principles of Six Sigma: a management philosophy created by the Motorola Company in 1980 and used by a multitude of companies worldwide. Many claim it's outdated. I have no opinion on that. I am not advocating Six Sigma but merely trying to draw parallels with a process many know, and stating how we humans, regardless of race or sex, and without any formal training, process a specific object.

I also add here that I have been talking about visual recognition, as it is the strongest sense of all. There are four other universally agreed upon senses: smell, hearing, taste and touch, which will be revisited when discussing the mind In Part 2.

Regarding power and control of oneself being the driving idea behind Focus, since the beginning of civilization, human beings, and yes, man in particular, have made it a ruthless and barbaric way of living and gaining their very real but still perceived control and power over others. From what history shows us about countries and cultures, and especially with their incredible understanding of patriotic/herd/mob mentality in order to get what they want, let's look at the many empires that have come and gone throughout history: Russian, Ming, Qing, Mughal and Mongol, Achaemenid/Persian, and the list goes on. Look at any of these and more, and you will see the same cycle: a nation of like-minded political and/or religious majority in peace, that eventually gets desensitized and desires more, leading them to takeovers in order to satisfy those desires. They establish and live based on an ideology, which is mutually accepted among their tribe/people.

There is also the flipside: a nation that is satisfied with what it has, yet now must change in order to protect itself from the aggression of aforementioned. It decides to turn violent to fight the unwanted aggression. What happens then? Again, the chicken or the egg? Which is which here, and do both sides not go through the same transmutation but via opposite catalysts/reasons?

Let us take a look at the ancient, brief, yet great Aztec Mesoamerican culture. It was a huge empire in what we now call Central America, and its final demise and destruction was at the hands of the Spanish Empire.

Prior to the 14th century, the Aztecs were poor hunter-gathers in Northern Mexico. For generations they wandered. One day they came upon Lake Texcoco. As legend has it, seeing an eagle eat a serpent was the symbol for them to stop. Geographically it seemed to be a land full of strategic richness, and they began to quickly grow as a nation.

In the 14th century, the Aztec empire was growing under numerous barbaric leaders. At the forefront was Moctezuma the 1st, yes, same as Montezuma. He was to become a brilliant 2nd Aztec empire ruler who knew how to use the absolutely brilliant minds to build the city, Tenochtitlan, on an island in the middle of Lake Texcoco. Under his reign the Aztec empire flourished through major expansion and partnerships with other tribes. This was a period of quasi-democratic strength, though under one ruler. There was a social, economic and political peace and cohesiveness during this period in the early 1400s. It was positive growth, even though there was much bloodshed, as these were barbaric days. (Remember this for later.)

To get to be the empire they had become, the Atzecs had to overcome plagues, locust invasions, famine, frosts, droughts, and floods. Lake Texcoco flooded the entire city. Their engineers designed a huge dyke spanning the lake. This dyke was the precursor to the 550 metre-long ICD (International Control Dam), which regulates the waters flowing over Niagara Falls. The Aztecs built a very similar dyke/dam, hundreds of metres long, complete with operating sluice gates — all out of natural products.

Human Mechatronics™: The Double-Edged Power of Influence

They organized, designed and created a 12-kilometre, multi-state aqueduct pipe system to bring an ample supply of fresh water to the states.

The engineers also devised ways of reproducing crops three to four times a year versus the normal one harvest. This gave the Tenochtitlans great strength and bargaining power. That brought them great riches but also great awareness to the outside world at a time when divide and conquer was a prime focus of other nations.

The droughts led to selling of children into slavery to buy food, and the city lost most of it people. Because of the famines, the Tenochtitlans believed the gods were upset. This was the start of an escalation in human sacrifices.

Peace ended for Moctezuma1 and his people. The Flower War, with much accumulation of victims to use as human sacrifices, began involving the Triple Alliance: three states partnering up: Tenochtitlan, Texacoco and Tlacopan. Growth and conquering other lands was paramount for their self-esteem and preservation. The bigger the better it seemed. Division of land within the Triple Alliance was not evenly spread. Tenochtitlan was still the boss. Remember that for what is about to come.

Moctezuma 1 died in 1469. A number of short reigns later, the eighth ruler, Ahuitzoti (pronounced: Witsot) took over in 1486. He was to become their greatest military leader. His first order of business was to suppress a Huastec rebellion. That was very paradoxical — bad that another tribe tried to take them over, but good that they stood up to and defended themselves; always more bloodshed.

In 1487, after the great Templo Mayor (pyramid-shaped city temple) was expanded upon, dedication included a 4-day celebration where thousands, if not tens of thousands, of humans were sacrificed by being thrown down the temple. Leader Ahuitzoti continued on this dramatically increased level of death through sacrifice as he doubled the size of the Aztec empire through ravaging and barbaric invasions. The empire was: powerful, rich in land and culture, rich in engineering creations, architecture, and very wealthy.

I hope you are enjoying this history lesson! ;-) Is it true that all good things come to an end?

Happening at the same time on the other side of the Atlantic Ocean, Spain had decided on their focus of vast divide and conquer. Once Columbus discovered the West Indies in 1492, eventually in 1519, Spaniard Conquistador Hernan Cortes landed an exploratory vessel in Central America and Tenochtitlan was the target.

Now under the rule of Moctezuma ll, Ahuitzoti's uncle, the Aztec empire was strong, but they had one other fear that would spell their demise. They feared the return of Quetzalcoati — the white bearded god who would take over their land (famine again). The white bearded Cortes knew this. Moctezuma ll was acknowledged to be a great leader by the Atzecs. He arranged a meeting with Cortes. He wanted to be kind and friendly. This worked at first, as Cortes reciprocated the gestures knowing about their god-belief.

Trust! How far does one go with trusting someone, some country, who is new and who is a stranger in your land?

And, to top that off, to the natives, the Spanish seemed like gods in appearance with their shiny armour, helmets and horses. The Aztecs were, as warriors, the cream of the crop in their territory but they would soon find out they weren't even close to the top in world comparison.

Through Moctezuma II's kind personality, he invited Cortes and his men into the capital, Tenochtitlan. This would be a tragic tactical error. Cortes had been secretly making alliances with those who hated the Aztecs. Once in the capital, the

Conquistadors took Moctezuma II captive, believing the Aztec people would not attack while their leader was prisoner. Cortes was wrong. The people had grown tired of Moctezuma II's kind ways trying to befriend the Spaniards, and attacked. First, however, as Spanish history has it, his own people attacked Moctezuma II. He died three days later. The Spaniards barely made it out alive.

After regrouping, coupled with the alliance they had made with local Aztec enemies, Cortez and his army came back with vengeance and slaughtered nearly the entire population in the capital.

After flourishing from 1345AD, in 1521, two years after the final battle with the Spanish Conquistadors and 176 years after the Aztecs started their growth, their empire was finally destroyed for good. (Source: National Geographic)

"Hate was just a legend,
And war was never known
The people worked together,
And they lifted many stones."
Cortez The Killer: Neil Young

Was it the devil with all the death leading the way or, was it the angel with all the growth that was in control? Would we have gotten to where we are today without this all happening?

What can we, today's modern, so-called superior world, draw parallels to and lessons from? After all, is that not what we are supposed to do; learn from the past, improve ourselves and become a better society through what our ancestors and previous world cultures have lived through?

What do you want to remember from this history, and how do you want to remember it? Those are two entirely different questions that allow for different answers based on who you are and how you see things. Yes, perception is part of this but let's assume everything about the Aztecs and Spaniards is true as noted above. What do you take away from this? How is today different? I'm going to leave those questions with you to ponder for the moment.

As a caveat to you answering how you want to remember it, remember this: because the Aztec empire was wiped out, much of the history is based on Spanish accounts. This is a lesson we need to understand; how one side in control with ultimate power can write the narrative to what is deemed to be reality, and probably even their ideology, and most everyone will believe it (wait until you read Chapter 4 on Scotoma).

Times have changed, right? Those were very barbaric times. We don't do that today, right?

Fast forward to April 26, 1937, and you have the Spanish (sorry to be picking on you, Spain. I really do love your country!) Civil War ending with the brutal bombing of the sacred Spanish town, Basques, Guernica by their own people, guided by Italy and Nazi Germany in support of Spanish General Franco's coup against the lawful government who were backed by the Soviet Union (Russia) at that time.

The almost three-year war itself was filled with terror, suffering, executions, murders, and assassinations. (Source: Britannica).

Check out Spain's own and internationally famous artist, the late Picasso and his famous monumental wall painting from that same year of 1937, "Guernica," to feel his sadness and revulsion over the war, and reasons behind it.

To understand politics, religion, cultural life/mindset, military, business, and labour force/workers involved in the wars is to understand the catalysts behind what actually starts a war — both globally and personally. It is also to understand what is happening in the world in 2020.

History always has a way of repeating itself because humans are afraid to learn for fear of feeling weak. We feel we already know better through sheer osmosis (absorbing the information) without putting those lessons into practice.

Chapter 2

Faith: The Stars, Religion, Politics

This title alone could be a book in itself. I'm sure it already is. We won't go too deep here but we need to set the base for how and why a particular "Living Order™" is part of the global "World Order" (how every nation works in tangent with each other to form the planet Earth's cohesive humanity), and how both "Orders" get established based on a developed and accepted faith. Why is this important? This is the original base of what was created to condition the people of the world - the cultures, sub-cultures, us, and you!

Faith, as a noun, defined by Oxford via Google is: "complete trust or confidence in someone or something." It is also: "a strong belief in God or in the doctrines of a religion, based on spiritual apprehension rather than proof."

To help understand how we think and how we are influenced, it is important to understand the origin of faith.

From day one of humankind, even before the previously mentioned two-individual (Adam & Eve, apes and/or cavemen) encounters, when any one of them opened their eyes, there must have been this sense of wonderment, fear, and curiosity. How did we get here? Who put us here?

This again is a missing link; it's what Darwin was trying to explain. Unless you believe in Darwinism, the first "creatures" were not babies. If they were, who gave birth to them? By many it is assumed that the first creatures on Earth were adults who then procreated. But how did those adults get here in the first place? There is still no definitive science with fact of any type that confirms any and all theories and/or beliefs.

Those individuals, in hopes of understanding why and how they were created and put on this strange land, looked to the largest and easiest place that was a mystery to them — the sky above. They questioned the heavens. The stars became a playground of imagination and fantasy.

Okay, now that we have that established, let's dive a bit deeper. As a kid I grew up with a book, written by Bruno Tomba, called *Stories of The Sky*. Groups of stars, or constellations, were created and defined, as stories that early travellers, say the Vikings, would use along with a significant star itself, to navigate through the seas. I even wrote a song called "Stories In The Sky" where I use the lines:

"A star shot through the darkened night
As Magellan sailed the seas
Vikings found their way back home
On a whisper of a breeze

A tale is told of ancient old
With stories in the sky
Time stand still and always will
With stories in the sky"

They started connecting the dots to form images. Thoughts and beliefs of the sky and its stars became divine/heavenly objects, which turned into a faith of ever-powerful beings. Ancient Roman and Greek mythology is fascinating!

Mythical stories, based on faith, supposed gods, and rationalization for being on Earth, were created and attached to the stars in forms of those constellations: Orion, Perseus, Andromeda, Pegasus, Virgo, The Archer, Big Bear, Little Bear, etc... Most were animals or god-like humans which many considered as sacred. Then, according to the months of visibility from "a" location on Earth, which makes this all somewhat biased, they connected the shapes to months of birth, creating the Zodiac and Horoscope, which has changed since then —as there were not the twelve months in a year that we use today.

Astronomy is "Science" while Astrology is "Legend" — without proof of influence (source: NASA), so it's important to explain the following. The Babylonians created the Zodiac, which more or less was the first real calendar, more than 3,000 years ago. They watched as the Earth circled the sun over a period of a year (very focused watching to be that precise). Different groups of stars, or constellations, would line up with the Earth's axis and were said to be, "in the zodiac." They divided the zodiac into twelve equal parts, assigning a constellation to each part. As the Earth orbited the sun, the sun would appear to pass through each of the twelve parts of the zodiac. The problem was that there were thirteen constellations, and the timeframes they used to assign to each was wrong. This new 13th constellation, called Ophiuchus (pronounced "O-few-cus"), is in between Scorpio and Sagittarius, shifting all others slightly to the left. This was verified based on new findings of the Earth's axis, by NASA in 2016. (source: Space.com)

Believe it or not, your sign, which many justify their entire life on, may be totally wrong — but you go ahead and keep believing in what you want. Regardless, they were created based on faith and imagination.

Even the calendar that the Babylonians created has gone through a multitude of changes from the Roman calendar reformed by Julius Caesar in 45 BC, then the 11th century Persian calendar, and finally the present-day Gregorian calendar created in 1582.

However, seeing as we are here now, with those accepted daily Horoscopes based on arguable Zodiac signs, once those faiths were created, then it came down to being grateful and making sure the gods were happy with us humans, and forming a set of rules that humans should live by to keep peace amongst the living but, more importantly, those divine watchers of endless power. Ergo religion and politics came next.

Religion is: how we philosophically/spiritually should live our lives, and how our immediate culture is to exist and survive —based on our belief and faith of our creation.

Politics is: under what kind of government (living order), rules and guidelines we follow on a daily basis to keep a type of order within the people.

Religion and politics are definitely intertwined. The rules and guidelines have been there over the ages to ensure all kept a nation's religious faith in place. Both can be tied to power: the wrong kind.

Politics, however, is everywhere else as well. There is politics in sports, in the arts, in a relationship. There can be politics between two people — between two people in love.

Individually, trying to live among the people of the world, these thoughts and beliefs hopefully roll unassumingly, without taking control of one's character and/or soul. However, you get a multitude, and then a majority of people believing the same thing, whether true or not, and regardless of concrete fact —that and the propaganda/brainwashing to form a Scotoma with it; it can soon become your new governing faith and/or religion changing who you are —to the core. And you never saw it coming because it was not of your own free mind. To this day, that process has not changed. We expand more on this soon.

Much has changed coming into this year of 2020 versus the 1960's and 70's. The children and young adults of today are the grandchildren and children of those parents from those past decades. Beliefs have changed with those times. Is that good or bad? Is it digression or evolution? Is it apathy or blind acceptance? Is it contempt or disdain versus respect?

Sadly, in my opinion, the times have taken a toll on religion. Here's where I may wrangle some feathers.

Human Mechatronics™: The Double-Edged Power of Influence

When I was growing up in the 1970's, there was a solid base of religion in my childhood years. For the record, I am United through blood and became Anglican via marriage. I came from a loving family that was very atypical back then: father worked; mother stayed home for the children. No judgement on that — I am just stating facts. I felt very fortunate with the church's approach. It was not extreme or in-your-face, nor did it feel pretentious or manipulative. It was very supportive and grounding, and I know that has helped give me strength to believe in myself and guide me to my current state of positive empowerment.

Over the years, however, there have been far too many scandals within the church that have tainted our security and beliefs. Many of these scandals have been based on either the church's abuse of power, government getting too involved, or individuals within the church and their abuse of power over others, in particular with sexual misconduct. That is very sad because religion and the church still has its place and need within the living orders. It's can be good to have like-minded people (tribe if you wish) to get energy from, to be inspired and motivated by and, to share faith with. Much of the younger generations, however, have grown up at home as latch-key (both parents work) children and through lack of parental grounding among others things, have lost connection to, and therefore faith in, religion.

I'm not sure which is better: these times or the past times of my youth. I try not to judge. I know the strength of my core and how empowered I feel based on the good, and acknowledging any bad, of my upbringing. I'm also a proud father who knows his role in how his children were raised with their own inner strength and free-thinking spirits. They have struggled, and will continue to struggle at times as we all do, but they were raised on not only a solid grounding, including faith and religion, but to also think for themselves, and I believe, and pray, that will give them strength to survive any struggle they encounter.

In summary, to keep order within a group of people with all different personalities, all different characteristics to their own nature of being, a set of guidelines is required. In other words, how we all behave cohesively, co-existing in a given living order, that becomes a set of rules. That is Government, which is Politics. It is also very much how individual relationships work.

Those rules should stay consistent but open to mutually evolving —even a nation's constitution, which was written centuries ago, should have room for change and growth.

However, there must be some way of holding people accountable for their own actions within those rules set forth — thus an oversight group, checks and balances, so it's not left to just one person's bias on how to form and manage, or govern over society's state of being that has been created through political power change.

Faith, religion, and politics are good, and very much needed to create stability, yet all can be threatened and abused by the Dark Side of Power. Never ever forget that! When there are enough people who disagree with what's been agreed upon by the group and decide to take action for no good reason except what they want to believe in; that's when dissention starts.

Is it for the good, or is it for the bad? People will say it's based on one's perception. I say it's also based on whether the morals, principles and ethics behind the change are contemptible or not. That is when protesting starts. It's when voices, not violence, are needed to express concern, fear and anger.

Considered one of the most influential Christian books of the 19th century, Lee Wallace wrote *Ben Hur: A Tale of the Christ* in 1880. It became a feature "silent" film in 1907 then again in 1925 both as precursors to the famous 1959 movie featuring Charlton Heston as Judah, Ben Hur. A quote taken from the book:

"There is no law by which to determine the superiority of nations; hence the vanity of the claim, and the idleness of

disputes about it. A people risen, run their race, and die either of themselves or in the hands of another, who, succeeding to their power, take possession of their place, and upon their monuments write new names; such is history."
   Lee Wallace

Chapter 3

Scotoma vs. Propaganda: Is It Your Mind or Someone Else's?

We are about to get into some deeper and more critical topics where many examples are used to illustrate how the outside influences affect us in response and belief, so, this chapter will be a bit long.

We will look at certain labels and their definitions. I am not a fan of labelling anyone based on their actions, yet we all do this when we ask why someone is behaving a certain way. We ask, "Why is he/she like that?" Psychology through the ages has used labels to categorize behaviours. I mention them here to stay consistent with society. The world would be better off if describing people and their challenges would be, "He suffers from mental illness" instead of "He is mentally ill." Maybe a better example might be, "She suffers from Schizophrenia" instead of "She's a Schizophrenic."

"Scotoma,": the etymology, taken from Wikipedia, is derived from the Ancient Greek "skotos" meaning "darkness"

"Scotoma,": the meaning, taken from Merriam-Webster Dictionary, being "a blind spot in the visual field in which vision is absent or deficient"

-symptoms may be mild and temporary, or leave some viewers with blind spots called scotomas, which may lead to migraine headaches.

According to Wikipedia, "every normal mammal eye (you and me) has a scotoma in its field of vision, usually termed its blind spot. This is a location with no photoreceptor cells, where the retinal ganglion cell axons that compose the optic nerve exit the retina. This location is called the optic disc. There is no direct conscious awareness of visual scotomas. They are simply regions of reduced information within the visual field. Rather than recognizing an incomplete image, patients with scotomas report that things "disappear" on them." Scotomas are often the result of damage to any part of the visual system, both accidentally and genetically. We may think we are perfect but we are far from it!

When a solar eclipse occurs, warnings are put out to the public, "do not look directly at the sun!" If you do, you will likely suffer a scotoma afterwards: a blind spot in your vision.

Welders are cautioned to wear designed shields to protect them from the intensity of the welding arc flash. Even then, it is so intense that many welders report "black spots" or "scotomas" in their vision.

As the author of this book, I'd like to share a revelation I experienced while researching and writing about the topic of scotoma while I was on my vacation on Terceira in the Azores Islands, one of nine Portuguese islands in the Mid-Atlantic.

I had been well aware of the term and meaning of scotoma, and its various off-shoots. As I dug deeper I discovered scintillating scotoma. This is something I have suffered with for most of my life. I could never really describe it.

According to Wikipedia, "Scintillating Scotoma," is a common visual aura preceding migraine and was first described by 19th-century physician Hubert Airy (1838-1923). It may precede a migraine headache, but can also occur acephalgically (without headache). It is often confused with retinal migraine, which originates in the eyeball or socket."

Human Mechatronics™: The Double-Edged Power of Influence

Eureka!!! I was so happy when I discovered this! It has been a huge distraction and mystery to me — to understand what this was. I had thought there was something wrong with me. At random I would start to sense this prism-shaped, jagged, encircling wavy line in my eyesight. If I closed my eyes, it was still there. If I turned my head or rolled my eyes, it was still there. In younger years I would have a migraine afterwards with a severe bruising feeling. In later years it would just be a bruising. It very well may have been my diet and my sugar levels that were the trigger; but it may have been stress as well.

It is true: self-education and learning only ends when you die.

Now, Psychological Scotoma: the meaning, taken from Medical Dictionary, in psychiatry, "is a figurative blind spot in a person's psychological awareness, the individual being unable to gain insight into and to understand his or her problems; lack of insight."

It has sometimes been described as a metaphor but it is more real that many would want to admit. In layperson's terms, it means: "The mind will believe what the mind wants to believe; regardless of facts and tangible evidence." It is a blind spot to reality. It is so important you understand this!

Now you ask, "What is reality?" This is potential for a BIG argument!

I enjoyed, immensely, the first *Matrix* movie in 1999. Starring Keanu Reeves as Neo and Laurence Fishburne as Morpheus, it is unique, albeit confusing at the time, entertainment. But, it is just that: entertainment —especially the lady in the red dress. The movie is about the reality of one's mind vs the reality of the world we live in.

Morpheus to Neo: "What you know you can't explain, but you feel it. You've felt it your entire life, that there's something wrong with the world. You don't know what it is, but it's there, like a splinter in your mind, driving you mad."

Okay, a lamp is a lamp. A car is a car. I am comfortable with my mind telling me that. It is universally accepted. We all call a car a car —we just use different languages to do so but it all means the same: a car, vehicle or automobile —just semantics! Etymology, or word origins, to be understood, needs to be studied more. It's actually a lot of fun.

The naysayer will argue, "It's only your mind that perceives it as a car. Ugh! No, this is, again, universally accepted for what it is. Otherwise we live in a fictional reality without any cohesiveness whatsoever and it will not function effectively at all.

That naysayer also says, "It was taken out of context." This is a line heard when a sentence is said and one word, usually, can change the meaning of what was said, such as, "I want you to do me a favour." That can mean many things but it's what precedes and follows, that defines, or manipulates, the context of the question. There is no denying what was said about "favour." People, however, use what's around it to make you believe it meant something else —to satisfy one's own needs. If you believe that — you are succumbing to Scotoma.

Psychological Scotoma is briefly mentioned in the book and movie, *Da Vinci Code* by Dan Brown. Again, "The mind will believe what the mind wants to believe, regardless of proven facts."

Once again from the movie, *The Matrix*,
Neo: "I thought it wasn't real."
Morpheus: "Your mind makes it real."

Create chaos and confusion, and then come in with strong conviction and powerful words —without the power of reasoning and true focus, the weak minds will jump on the bandwagon and follow.

This is where a quasi-democratic society, as I noted with the Aztecs, prevails. The ruler was voted in, and in ancient times (nepotism — those with power or influence favouring relatives or friends for jobs, was rampant even then), many subsequent rulers started by being heirs to the throne. Even these days, he or she is voted in and will strive for executive privilege (to not be held to group rules). In other words, they will decide themselves what is right for the country, ignoring any democratic discussion with the government for oversight. This borders on dictatorship. Double-speak becomes common-place as in politics one party is trying to find connections to sway all sides in order to get more votes. Take this too far, and society flirts with becoming Orwellian in nature. Once you taste that controlling power, you want more. Once you get more, you want it all.

"Propaganda," the meaning taken from Oxford via Google, "is information, especially of a biased or misleading nature, used to promote a political cause or point of view."

It's not just in politics —it's everywhere, with everything. Much of sales and marketing involves some form of propaganda. It's all about convincing someone to think a certain way so they want something. Sales and marketing isn't necessarily misleading, but it is about directing one's focus on specific parts of what is being sold/offered and often doesn't come with full disclosure of the item and its shortcomings.

To put it simply, propaganda is used to brainwash people; to make them think a certain way. Propaganda is usually of a very repetitive nature with a simple goal of changing one's paradigm to mimic the storyteller's.

Taken from Oxford via Google, "Paradigms,": are generally defined as a framework that has unwritten rules and that directs action. A paradigm shift occurs when one paradigm loses its influence and another takes over." It is how we as individuals live within a routine throughout our lives. We humans so desperately want routine that we often allow outside influence to rule our individual way of "being." At times we want to latch onto someone who shows success. Social media is a reflection of this with people "liking" to death celebrities or people of so-called high popularity. The marketing industry, or storytellers, knows this all too well.

Sometimes we embrace these celebrities with blind love. It's human nature to want to latch onto something, someone who emits positive vibrations and who seems well liked. Sometimes we need them so much in order to feel better ourselves that we put them on a pedestal with over-the-top adulation where we feel they can do no wrong. However, when that very person who became our hero does something seriously wrong, or even just different from what is normally accepted, we turn a blind eye and accept them regardless of reality — whereas with most others, we would judge and condemn. Whether as an individual or a part of a group, we would be so quick to turn on someone should they falter. But, that is the difference when one has gained hero/legend status. There the paradox exists.

To tie scotoma and propaganda together, let's take a look at some sports celebrities: Colin Kaepernick — former National Football League (NFL) quarterback for one. Then how about we look at Wade Boggs, Jeff Gordon, Michael Jordan, Brett Favre and Tiger Woods vs Pete Rose.

I write this part ironically on February 2, 2020: the date that makes a very cool and rare palindrome: 02022020, Ground Hog Day (both Pennsylvania's Punxsutawney Phil and Canada's Wiarton Willie today predicted an early spring), and it's Super Bowl Sunday where Kansas City Chiefs play the San Francisco 49ers, of whom Colin Kaepernick was once the star quarterback and who led San Francisco to the 2012-2013 season Super Bowl Championship, where they were beaten by the Baltimore Ravens.

In 2015 and 2016, Colin, being an activist, started taking a more serious and public stance to protest what he believed were serious injustices. During the national anthem prior to the start of a game in 2016, he, with a couple team-mates, began to take a knee to the ground while everyone else was doing the customary standing. The protest was for awareness of the racial injustice and systematic oppression in the United States.

That's good, is it not? Controversial in the moment - maybe yes for some. Racial injustice and systematic oppression, however, are not good in a democratic world, so speaking up is good, right? We need to create awareness. We need to protest. How Colin did that, however, created a very polarized nation which, had fuel thrown on when its President buttedinterjected in and decided to micromanage by telling all the powers-that-be that they should fire anyone who protested like that —including Colin.

How would you feel if an Authoritarian leader told you how to think? To the outside world, we see a shepherd leading the flock. Are you okay being the sheep?

"Authoritarianism," the meaning taken from Oxford via Google, is "the enforcement or advocacy of strict obedience to authority at the expense of personal freedom." And what happens if you do not obey? You get outcast, fired, cheated on, downgraded in job level, all for serving the people instead of just one person. How would "you" feel if you were chastised the same way for your seemingly harmless beliefs?

Since then, with that extra help/push, Colin has been blacklisted from professional football with a current attempt to vanquish his legacy into today's 2020 Super Bowl game featuring his ex-team.

Wade Boggs: Former baseball third baseman mainly for the Boston Red Sox, All-Star, World Series Champion, voted third best moustache in baseball, husband and father to two children with wife, Debbie, beloved by many baseball fans who watched him play, Hall of Fame inductee: famous for extra-marital affair with Margo Adams.

Jeff Gordon: Legendary race car driver, Rookie of the Year in different divisions, four-time NASCAR Cup Series Champion, 2012 Heisman Humanitarian Award, named in Top 50 NASCAR all-time drivers, first marriage with (Jennifer) Brooke Sealey-Gordon from 1994-2002, born-again-Christian starting in mid-1990's, Philanthropist, National Midget Auto Racing Hall of Fame, Motorsports Hall of Fame, NASCAR Hall of Fame: famous for extra-marital affair in 2001 with Playboy model Deanna Merryman, which led to his divorce while being born-again.

Michael Jordan (MJ, Air Jordan): Legendary and arguably the greatest professional basketball player to have played the game, Chicago Bulls star, Multiple All-Star awards, the name "Jordan" has become synonymous with great basketball playing, arguably the greatest sports marketing program ever by Nike, 14x-time NBA All-Star, 3x-NBA All-Star game MVP, 6x-NBA Finals MVP, 5x-NBA MVP, 6x NBA Champion including 3x in a row — twice, 9x-All NBA Defensive First Team, Rookie of the Year, 2x-NBA Slam-Dunk Contest Winner, 14x-NBA Scoring Leader, NCAA Champion, NBA's 50th Anniversary All-Time Team, Presidential Medal of Freedom, NBA Hall of Fame 1st Ballet, Husband and Father to two sons and one daughter with first wife, Juanita Vanoy from 1989-2002: famous for extra-marital affair with multitudes of women which led to divorce, yet idolized and cherished endlessly by the fans.

Brett Favre: American Football great. Former Quarterback with the Green Bay Packers, first quarterback to pass for 500 touchdowns, throw for 70,000 yards, complete 6,000 passes, and attempt 10,000 passes, Super Bowl Champion, 11x Pro Bowl, 3x

Human Mechatronics™: The Double-Edged Power of Influence

1st Team All-Pro, 3x 2nd Team All-Pro, 3x NFL Most Valuable Player, Sports Illustrated Sportsman of the Year, Green Bay Packers No. 4 retired, Packers Hall of Fame, NFL 1990s All-Decade Team, NFL 100th Anniversary All-Time Team, father of two daughters, grand-father to one, married to breast cancer survivor and author Deanna Favre, and was threatened to leave more than once by his wife because of his "inappropriate behaviour with women, alcohol binges, and Vicodin abuse" (source: Don't Bet Against Me by Deanna Favre) and, allegedly was unfaithful while sexting with: Sports Illustrated Columnist, Gameday hostess, gracing both Maxim and Playboy, and wife's doppelganger, Jenn Sterger. To Sterger's credit, she refused his advances.

Tiger Woods: For a long time from the late 1990s and well into the 2000s, Tiger was the top-rated golfer in the world (683 weeks in a row). He is arguably the most famous athlete of all (if instead he was known as Eldrick Woods with no Tiger; would he still be so famous? Smart self-branding). 11x winner of: PGA Player of the Year, 4x winner of all four golf majors: 4x PGA Championship, 3x winner of The U.S. Open, 5x winner of The Masters, 3x winner of The British Open, holder of the "Tiger-Slam" (Champion of all four Majors at the same time but not in same year); as of 2019 winner of 82 PGA golf tournaments tying him with the legendary Jack Nicklaus for #1 all-time, Multi-year winner of: PGA Tour Player of the Year, Leading money winner, Vardon Trophy, Byron Nelson Trophy, Fed-Ex Cup Champion and, awarded Presidential Medal of Freedom. Father to two children with Elin Nordegren who he was at one time a devoted husband with until in 2009 it came out that Tiger had numerous extra-marital affairs with countless women over many years. Yet today, in 2020, the jumping onto the bandwagon by the masses chanting, "Tiger, Tiger, Tiger", and, "You da man!" are still very real.

We can even include some Hollywood celebrities: Arnold Schwarzenegger, Jude Law, Ashton Kutcher, Meg Ryan, Marilyn

Monroe, Elizabeth Taylor, Kristen Stewart and Hugh Grant to name a few of the multitude guilty of extra-marital affairs.

How about musicians? Let's not go there except to mention arguably the father of the blues, Robert Johnson, LeAnn Rimes and Jay-Z. (Source for information on athletes, actors and musicians - Wikipedia)

Somewhere along the way, much of society forgot that marriage, and even a committed relationship, is a partnership. That partnership includes, among many things, a business operation.

To paraphrase the late Stephen Covey as he described his three habits in his book, *The 7 Habits of Highly Effective People*, Independence: I am an individual, I am myself —I can get what I want through my own efforts; Dependant: I need others (you) for various things I cannot achieve by myself; Interdependence: is about multiple (even just two) people being mutually dependent on one another and combining their own efforts with the efforts of others (you), achieve their greatest success.

A husband and wife, (see, we/some have evolved for the good — it used to be "man and wife") a married couple, a committed relationship — are all partnerships that need to be based on love, which includes respect and honesty. You have your role; I have mine. We are a great team! But then temptation is around us all, and we all want to be wanted and admired with that exciting flame and desire we once felt. Scotoma!

From the movie *Little Women*, based on the 1868-1869 book by Louisa May Alcott:

Amy March to Laurie Laurence: "So don't sit there and tell me that marriage isn't an economic proposition, because it is. It may not be for you, but it certainly is for me."

Taken at face value, this quote may very well fit the above paragraph —not as a reason behind marriage, or partnership, but as a topic of discussion for a healthy partnership. It is a topic where fear enters in, not wanting to sound selfish. Combine this quote with the rest of Amy's statement, it changes everything and is very harsh and sexist when trying to fit with today's gender equality. But, this was only said for show business and entertainment - we hope ;-)

We "keep" the individuals in the aforementioned lists on a pedestal because we need to believe in their fame and infamy. Their accomplishments, for some of us, are as real today as they were decades ago, and it keeps us feeling young, and alive. We want to believe in them. We want to have someone to look up to; to be inspired by, so much that sometimes we look away from the truth.

The reality is, by sexually cheating with someone else, they have committed the very sin that would hurt us the most: betraying the one they have committed to and agreed to love — exactly the very thing we all cherish the most. Are we thinking for and being honest with ourselves?

> "What are those voices outside love's open door
> Make us throw off our contentment,
> And beg for something more?"
> Heart of the Matter by Don Henley (Eagles)

Then, there is, in my opinion, the double standard of Pete Rose, aka "Charlie Hustle," former professional baseball player and manager, who as a third baseman and switch-hitter achieved the following: 17x All-Star, 3x World Series Champion, World Series MVP, Rookie of the Year, 2x Gold Grove winner, Silver Slugger Award, Roberto Clemente Award, 3x NL Batting Champion, Retired #14 from Cincinnati Reds, Cincinnati Hall of Fame, Major League Baseball All-Century Team and holds the #1 Record in Major League Baseball: career hits: 4,256 career singles: 3,215; career games played: 3,562; career at bats: 14,053; and career plate appearance: 15,890. His talent and success as a professional baseball player are undeniable, yet he has been branded for life and barred from ever being inducted to the Baseball Hall of Fame for doing what many enjoy doing:

gambling on sports. Just like Mike (MJ — Michael Jordan), who also famously gambled on sports.

I am not here to condone his/their actions. There is a code of conduct to follow and abide by. That is the religion and politics of sports. The penalties, however, sometimes cross over into sheer hypocrisy with double standards.

Why is it that humans end up condoning, idolizing and maintaining that gloriously high pedestal for those guilty of something that hurts us to the core, something that people go into deep depression over and even take their own life because they can't stand the pain of this type of betrayal through infidelity? Yet, someone who breaks a singular particular code by doing something a majority of society does, whether it's through a sports lottery or a bet between friends, gets banished for "life" from celebrating the accomplishments achieved both individually and for his team.

Writing a false narrative is all part of that. Remember, we humans always seek something familiar — something comfortable. We do and why not? I do! Our mind latches onto comfort. We have to remember though that we are in control of what and how deeply the outside world goes into our conscious mind, as well as how we process and absorb that information (more on this in Part 2: Human Mechatronics™).

If something is repeated enough to us, our mind "can" start to believe it all — which can form that paradigm we discussed earlier. If taken to obsessive levels, it's easy to forget about reality and truth. That's where we humans can develop that scotoma, right? I am emphasising the word "can," because you are in control of your mind. That is what these books are all about. What external influences are programming you?

The brain vs the mind: wired vs programmed. We also discuss this later but it's crucial that you are aware right now of that possibility.

Here are some famous cases of propaganda: true or false?

- 1917-German Cadaver (Corpse) Factory: It is one of the most atrocious propaganda stories that was believed in and which had major future consequences. To make ammunition during World War 1, the nitro glycerine needed fat from animals. After the British set up a blockade to limit trade to stall the Germans, animals were suddenly in a decline. The news was out that the Germans, with reducing animal fat, instead burnt the Jewish and then their own dead to use the human fat to make that ammunition.

    Fact or fiction? In 1925, British Brigadier-General John Charteris admitted it was a hoax, which he later retracted. Why? Did politics intervene in the truth? Then later in 1941, during World War II, Hitler supposedly used those propaganda stories to create real cadaver factories. Historians say 1917 was false but 1941 was actually true. I have no idea. It's an amazingly sad and surreal story but to the world at that time, the propaganda formed a national physiological scotoma and helped create the history we today have evolved from.

Other propaganda stories:

- Did America actually land on the moon first or was it a set-up so America could claim victory in the space race against the USSR-Russia? The controversy continues through today.

- Did "only" John Wilkes Booth assassinate John F Kennedy or was it a CIA set-up with multiple people involved? Is governmental propaganda brainwashing us to believe what they want us to believe?

- Did Jimi Hendrix die from choking on his vomit or did the CIA set it up due to Jimi's increased level of influence being connected to the Black Panther Group? Are we again being brainwashed by government to believe the first scenario?

- Viennese psychologist Ernest Dichter was very instrumental in the 1950s and 60s, helping corporate America understand marketing. He performed a survey of housewives circa 1955 for food maker Betty Crocker, who had started quick and easy cake mixes. All you needed to do is add water and bake. The product did not sell. Enter Dichter, who arguably determined that the women felt they didn't deserve that kind of product because it was too easy and the lack of work brought on guilt. Whether scientifically needed or not, Betty Crocker decided to add one step to the process: add an egg. The women now felt involved and worthy. Sales of the cake mix soared, as did the Betty Crocker company. One egg, again whether needed or not, changed the future of advertising.

- There is the Wendy's Restaurant logo with the word "mom" at the top of the girl's (founder Dave Thomas' daughter) blouse collar. The original logo didn't really depict this at all. The logo changed in 1983 to mainly tweak the girl's pigtails and refresh the image. In 2013 the latest logo appeared with the word, "MOM" much more clearly defined. What do you think — propaganda or just smart subliminal marketing?

    "Subliminal marketing," the meaning taken from Oxford via Google is, "a stimulus or mental process below the threshold of sensation or consciousness; perceived by or affecting someone's mind without their being aware of it." This has been powerful ever since the 1960s. Actually, the focus on marketing started way back in 1895 with the psychologist,

Human Mechatronics™: The Double-Edged Power of Influence

Harlow Gale, and then later escalated hugely by, and even of late, Robert Cialdini.

Along with aforementioned Ernest Dichter and the cake mix egg, there is Austrian Edward Bernays, who many consider the "father" of propaganda and advertising. I thank my oldest child for reminding me of the "influence Bernays had on the conscious mind along with the intelligent manipulation of the organized habits and opinions of the masses. It is an important element in today's so-called democratic society." This quote is taken from his 1928 groundbreaking book entitled *Propaganda*. He promoted the term, "public relations" and was hired by many of America's major companies to design psychological programs to help "control and regiment the masses according to our will "without" their knowledge of it." He was directly connected to the Whitehouse and instrumental behind Calvin Coolidge's 1924 election victory for President of the United States. To further understand his influence on the world, which remains in effect even today, I strongly urge you to read *Propaganda* to understand why we think the way we do when it comes to marketing. Even the German Nazis used Bernays' writings to influence the public; the Cadaver Factories story, whether fact or fiction, may very well have originated through his works.

Early examples also include the Benson & Hedges 100's cigarette pack graphics with the young man hugging the attractive blond woman. Research says that the backbone of the woman is reshaped to appear as an erect male phallus, yes that means a penis, which is supposed about to enter into the woman's hair curls, subliminally portrayed as a vagina. I didn't see this the first time looking at it. But, and a big but, they have now put the imagery in my mind. If I allow it to be absorbed into the subconscious mind through the repetitive viewing, then I believe it. Even if I don't, it has entered my mind and I will think of it.

In the 1960s there was research done where advertisers would inject an image that lasted not even a quarter of a second (part of subliminal messaging). It was not visible to the conscious mind as it was so quick. Repeat this over and over and over, and the mind starts to acknowledge it as the truth. (Source for aforementioned propaganda specifics and statistics: Wikipedia)

Today, marketing is rampantly abused through social media and television. It preys on fears and desires. Imagery is so real and connected with our hormones that it has an incredible effect on us humans; just they way they planned.

That's what sales and marketing is! And that's what religion and politics is all about too; finding ways to get the masses to believe in someone's belief, and there is almost always money and power tied to it.

Right here, right now, accept the fact that there are multitudes of people, companies, cultures, countries and faiths that will go to many lengths in order to manipulate and influence human behaviour, a.k.a. YOU, for their own benefit.

Remember, this book is written to bring this all to your awareness and give you the tools to help you stay in control of your own thoughts and focus, and live "your" life to its fullest and most positive!

Jack Nicholson in the 1992 movie *A Few Good Men*, also starring Demi Moore and Kevin Bacon, delivered the explosive and iconic line to the attorney, Jack, played by Tom Cruise:

"You want the truth!?"
"You can't handle the truth!"

We want to believe in "a" truth but at what cost? The truth is also what we fear! Do you know the difference between what's true and what's fake, and can you handle it if it's not what you like?

Chapter 4

Narcissism vs. Pride + Self-Esteem + Charisma

Before we dive deeper into that last statement from Mr. Nicholson, and the cognitive behaviours behind it, let's understand what drives or motivates people.

This is going to be another long chapter. Stay with me through it all. It all comes together in Parts 3 and 4.

We humans (I dare say most living creatures) all want, or desire, three fundamental core needs: survival, freedom, and to feel we matter — to someone — to mean something for being brought to the reality of being! Yes we do! There may be many other things we want, but these three make up the core.

Whatever your race or nationality is, whatever colour or gender you are, whatever religion you believe in (if any), or whatever political colours you wear, those three core needs are universally humanistic "wants" or "desires!"

Let's break this statement down further.

"Survival." Before we are even born, our brains are wired for survival! Fear is a large part of that. When we see something we cannot explain, we go through those steps of "first meeting" laid out in Chapter One: acknowledging, analyzing, recognizing, defining, and measuring — our automatic defences activate. Then it's the "fight or flight" decision our mind performs for us, especially if we struggle with the "recognize" part. The mind wants us to survive.

Survival:
Survival to physically live and not die
Survival to be happy with how we live on this world, in the culture we are in — with our "self"
Survival to live the best we can with "Freedom"

Freedom comes in many variations all within and as a working part of your Living Order.
Freedom:
Freedom of living: You are able to live your day, without concern of any penalty.
Freedom of movement: You are able to move within your day as you wish, and having dealt with "original" or "evolved" limitations. An example of this would be someone who has to use a wheelchair, or someone with phocomelia (born with no limbs — Chapter #18 on Distractions).
Freedom of speech: You are able to say, hopefully with a level of respect, what's on your mind without fear of retribution.
Freedom of choice: You are able to choose what you want to do based on your personal desires.
Freedom of mind: You are able and allowed to think as you wish, being cognizant (mindfully self-aware) of your choice of your own free will, with sound wisdom of being either hurtful or helpful to the world, and knowing why you choose what you do.

Scotoma can play a huge part in these last two: choice and mind. I will bring this all together in the Chapter #9, The World Order.
To Matter:
Human beings want to matter in many ways:
To matter by feeling we are on this Earth for a purpose.
To matter to someone, where they care about us.
To matter to something (a cause, a career, a group) so we can feel we fit in and are accepted by a larger order.

Human Mechatronics™: The Double-Edged Power of Influence

Most of all, to matter to our "self" in order to believe in our existence.

All three are also connected to states we reach with our mind. All three overlap very much in our everyday living. Survival and freedom are senses associated and controlled partly by our actions. To matter, however, is all based on how we think, and can be destructive to the other two. Should one or more of these "desires" be threatened, that's when our self-esteem is affected and our "self" changes — sometimes for the good, and all too often for the bad.

I recently read a post on Facebook that resonated with me,
"Only people who are not happy with themselves are mean to others."
What do you think about that? What does being "happy" truly mean? One can be happy on the surface because they have let themselves believe in their current state of reality, but in truth, they have a deep, inner anger, or even hatred, which is the basis of their living. This was Ringo from the movie *Tombstone* that I referred to at the beginning of this book.

"Self-esteem," the meaning taken from Wikipedia, is "an individual's subjective evaluation of one's own worth. Self-esteem encompasses beliefs about oneself as well as emotional states, such as triumph, despair, pride and shame." Having a positive self-esteem is when charisma can kick in.

"Low self-esteem," the meaning taken from Psychalive, "is characterized by lack of confidence and feeling badly about oneself. People with low self-esteem often feel unlovable, awkward, or incompetent. They have a fragile sense of self that can easily be wounded (and manipulated) by others. Furthermore, people with low self-esteem are hyper-vigilant and hyper-alert to signs of rejection, inadequacy, and rebuff."

No one wants to experience feeling low self-esteem — ever!

To challenge this is to say that from the day we were born, we are okay with feeling incompetent — that we are okay and accept feeling unconfident, unlovable, untrusting and awkward. I do not believe anyone was ever born "wanting" those feelings.

It is: negative energy, experience, conditioning by others including society itself, coupled with the lack of encouragement and support from people whom we expect to love us unconditionally, and also from complete strangers, as well as those self-evolving sad feelings we allow to pass through our conscious mind, that tear down any positive self-esteem we had as an infant. This is what we will learn to control.

Some will argue that low self-esteem can be inbred or congenital; in other words, having a particular trait from birth or by firmly established habit.

To be born with a genetic predisposition "from birth?" I agree. My belief in the creation of a human being — for that matter, any living form — is that there is an established "standard" (what makes the human body and all its systems) plus a diverse arrangement composing the aggregate of "substance" (electrical components), including souls (the software/brain) which goes into each sperm cell and fertile egg. When they meet and combine, they create "You" — a truly unique and living being. More on this in Human Mechatronics™ — Part 2.

With that belief, yes, the genes of low self-esteem can be there at birth, along with other traits: kind and not so kind.

Can it be reversed? For what I believe would be a majority of people, I answer absolutely, "YES!" Many can be reprogrammed, which is not quite the same as "rewired, which involves genetics and DNA. Let's say "Yes" to "modified." Sounds like I'm talking about a machine, right? We are Human Machines! Do not ever lose sight of that!

Many people want to be modified! Thus, the billions of dollars spent each year on self-help. This is where the terms, "paradigm change", "paradigm shift", or "establish from habit" have become increasingly popular. It's all about growth in a supposed positive direction.

Human Mechatronics™: The Double-Edged Power of Influence

"Established from habit?" "Low self-esteem?" A firmly established habit is a paradigm that has taken repetition and time to form into the person's M.O. (Modus Operandi) — way of being.

"Way of being!" What is that? There are people who stay in the background and just carry on best they can with little engagement of the world. That is their way of being. There are people who engage and mix in easily with the world yet appear very comfortable with themselves and don't need to stand out and force themselves. Then there are those who seem to take any opportunity to be front and centre on stage where all can see. Which one are you? How do you feel about your way of being? None of the above necessarily leads to self-esteem issues. On the contrary, these "ways of being" can be great, unless the following gets out of both balance and control. For many who have experienced higher education with colleges and universities as their first time independently out in the world, being part of "that" type of living order can force oneself into uncomfortable and uncharacteristic situations, especially if one is a member of a fraternity. It can bring life-changing events - both positive and negative for the soul.

Let's take a look at pride, narcissism and charisma, which are all different yet can, unfortunately, be too closely tied to each other.

"Pride," the meaning taken from Oxford via Google, is "a feeling or deep pleasure or satisfaction derived from one's own achievements."

It's okay to feel proud about something. This is a good thing, a good feeling. We humans want to stretch ourselves and reach higher levels. That is a natural desire and test we create with our minds — to know we can do better. When we do, we feel proud, and rightfully so. It's a feeling we have for our "self," but it can also be for and about others.

"Narcissism," the meaning taken from Oxford via Google, is "an excessive interest in or admiration of oneself and one's physical appearance. Traits also include selfishness, involving a sense of entitlement, a lack of empathy, and a need for admiration. There is a self-centredness arising from failure to distinguish the self from external objects, either in very young babies or as a feature of mental disorder." It is a self-induced attitude regardless of consciously being aware of it or not.

"Charisma," is a state of natural being. The meaning, taken from Oxford via Google, "compelling attractiveness or charm that can inspire devotion by others."

"Charm," the meaning taken from Oxford via Google, is the root of charisma. The meaning is a natural, "power or quality of giving delight or arousing admiration."

The last two parts of each of these definitions — "can inspire devotion by others" and "arousing admiration" — open a door that is often a beacon light for those wanting power, and is where narcissists will feel their best. They realize that it is becoming all about them, and this feeds their fire to want more control. They need attention! They need to see and feel the fame, being viewed as the very — if not the most important, and that way their low self-esteem is boosted by their abuse of others.

This is synonymous with some phrases that are increasingly used today, especially with the young, and especially in business: The "Type A" and the "Alpha Personality;" AF = Alpha Female; AM: Alpha Male vs. its counterpart, the AM: Beta Male. The "Alpha" label is a term that people almost wear with pride to justify that they have to do whatever they need to in order to get what they want — regardless of who they hurt and how unethical they are.

In case you were wondering, the meaning of Alpha (slang) Male type personality, taken from Dictionary.com via Google, "refers to a dominant person or their behaviour, especially with respect to social aggressive, hyper-masculine men."

Alpha Women are defined as "powerful and successful women, often in a leadership role. Alpha females are often described as intimidating by men and women alike."

Type A personality is different in that it is psychological instead of behavioural.

A Beta male personality, taken from the Urban Dictionary, is "someone who lacks the masculinity alpha male. They are non-confrontational and are unable to assert masculine dominance."

A Beta female, taken from the Urban Dictionary, is the Alpha Female's right hand woman. A beta will be one of the Alpha female's closest friends and one of her most trusted confidants. The Beta is second in command and knows when to keep silent and when to talk. A Beta is never an Alpha wannabe; she is comfortable with who she is."

Charm and charisma are actually two descriptions of very positive and confident personalities. Narcissism is certainly seen as being negative due to its self-centredness, arrogance, and me first attitude.

Mix all three of these together into one person and it can be very scary. Being with someone like this — charismatic, full of charm and narcissistic traits — will likely be toxic for anyone closely associated. Oh, it will be fun, contagious and exciting. They are usually very intelligent and knowledgeable, they can talk circles around many and make one feel great, but then suddenly you feel like you are the stupid one and "the" problem in the relationship. There is a method to the attack. Being with a narcissist, one can lose who they are. You love the charm and charisma until it takes you over. Then what? You love it but hate it. You want to run but the charm makes you feel good so you stay, even though you know better.

Reports say that narcissism personality traits have reached epidemic levels. Narcissistic people will never agree with this statement. Why? Because they believe their way is the only way, and they are usually in denial of how they present themselves. They don't care. This is a book unto itself in that it is so deep a subject, especially when delving into Narcissistic Personality Disorder (NPD), not to be confused with Borderline Personality

Disorder (BPD). I will leave those two to the specialized experts in their fields as I fully understand and appreciate their complexity.

This is not meant to be a political book; however, we must understand a certain level of politics: philosophies, characteristics, methods, influence and propaganda if we are to buy into leaders saying this is how we are to be and think — without us suffering from Psychological Scotoma. In other words, with reason and our own free will, we choose to support based on our own free and clear minds.

There is also politics in a relationship; and the difference is only in size. Is there a "head" of your household? Relationship Behaviour, at its basic core, can be sadly the same.

Every leader deals with power. Every leader deals with influencing human beings. Every leader deals with controlling people. Call it want you want: Leaders have power, and much of the time have only a vague idea of how to properly use it — at least in the beginning. That's why there are rules in place to work with established support teams.

The following are some terms that are useful to know. They are all used within the political arena; however, they are also part of personality traits within human relationships:

"Machiavellian," (Maa-kee-uh-**vel**-lee-uhn) the meaning taken from Oxford via Google, is "cunning, scheming, and unscrupulous, especially in politics."

According to *Psychology Today* and *Scientific American*, the term, "Dark Triad" was coined by Delroy Paulhus and Kevin Williams in the *Journal of Research in Personality* in 2002. It involves three negative personality traits: narcissism, psychopathy, and Machiavellianism. Dark Triad and Dark Side are very similar in nature.

This is opposite to "Light Triad" involving three positive personality traits: Humanism (valuing the dignity and worth of each individual), Kantianism (treating people as ends unto themselves, not mere means), and Faith in Humanity (believing in the fundamental goodness of humans).

Machiavellianism is rarely heard within general public conversations; however, when understanding negative cognitive behaviour, it cannot be overstated.

"Gaslighting" is a term gathering significant momentum in current days. The meaning taken from Oxford via Google: "manipulate (someone) by psychological means and questions their own sanity." Many who have found them on the bad/surprise side of infidelity understand what this word implies to one's emotions.

"Cunning," the meaning taken from Oxford via Google: "having or showing skill in achieving one's ends by deceit or evasion."

"Scheming," the meaning taken from Oxford via Google: "given to or involved in making secret and underhand plans."

"Unscrupulous," the meaning taken from Oxford via Google: "a person having or showing no moral principles; not honest or fair."

"Politics A," the meaning taken from Oxford via Google, is "the activities associated with the governance of a country or area, especially the debate between parties having power."

"Politics B," taken from Oxford via Google, is "the activities aimed at improving someone's status or increasing power within an organization."

"Organization," taken from Oxford via Google, is "an organized group of people with a particular purpose."

"Xenophobia": taken from Oxford via Google, is "dislike or prejudice against people from other countries.

"Homophobia," taken from Oxford via Google, is "a range of negative attitudes and feelings toward homosexuality or people who are identified or perceived as being lesbian, gay, bisexual or transgender and questioning."

I know I may be pushing this but we might as well add a few more that fall into play within politics:

"Brainwashing," the meaning taken from Oxford via Google: "the process of pressuring someone into adopting radically different beliefs by using systematically and often forcible means."

"McCarthyism," the meaning taken from Oxford via Google, is "the practice of making accusations of subversion or treason without proper regard for evidence."

"Democracy," the meaning taken from Oxford via Google is "a system of government by the "whole" population or all the eligible members of a state, typically through elected representation."

"Paradox/Contradiction," the meaning taken from Oxford via Google, is "a statement or proposition that, despite sound (or apparently sound) reasoning from acceptable premises, leads to a conclusion that seems senseless, logically unacceptable, or self-contradictory."

"Liberalism," the meaning taken from Oxford via Google is, "a political and moral philosophy based on liberty, consent of the government and equality before the law."

"Oppression," the meaning taken from Oxford via Google, is "prolonged cruel or unjust treatment or control. Mental pressure or distress."

"Conservatism," the meaning taken from Oxford via Google, is "commitment to traditional values and ideas with opposition to change or innovation." It also means, "the holding of political views that favour free enterprise, private ownership, and socially conservative ideas."

"Sacrosanct," the meaning taken from Merriam-Webster, is "a process or action that is treated as sacred or holy: immune from criticism or violation."

"Fascism," the meaning taken from Oxford via Google, is "a form of far-right authoritarianism ultra nationalism characterized by dictatorial power, forcible suppression of opposition, and strong regimentation of society and of the economy which came to prominence in early 20th-century

Europe" and is possibly evolving in other countries."

"Left-wing politics," the meaning taken from Google, is "supports social equality and egalitarianism, often in opposition to social hierarchy. It typically involves a concern for those in society whom its adherents perceive as disadvantaged relative to others as well as a belief that there are unjustified inequalities that need to be reduced or abolished."

"Right-wing politics," the meaning taken from Google, is "holds that certain social orders and hierarchies are inevitable, natural, normal or desirable, typically supporting this position on the basis of natural law, economics, or tradition."

"Far-right," the meaning taken from Google, is "politics further on the right of the left-right spectrum than the standard political right, particularly in terms of "extreme" nationalism, native ideologies, and authoritarian tendencies."

"Far-left," the meaning taken from Google, is "politics further on the right of the left-right spectrum than the standard political right."

Where, now, do these other terms, or labels, fit in: entitlement, extremist, supremacist, and anarchist or anarchy? With the increasing political polarization within individual nations, these are all extreme right-wing terminologies to describe the actions and attitudes of those who protest and rely on herd, or mob groups of people to fight against the existing living order. Mix these into real life and people get hurt and even killed. These attitudes of hatred, artificially formed via scotoma, to boost the individual's low self-esteem through finding the feeling of misguided power that was described in the beginning of this book, are driving philosophies behind terrorism and gang violence.

One more definition:

"Gullible" the meaning taken from Oxford via Google, is a person "easily persuaded to believe something credulous. They believe what other people say, and does what others ask without thinking."

So why was all this not in the chapter on politics? It's because, in today's world, narcissism has become too much of a factor in the leadership of many a nation. I tried to describe, in hopefully simple terms, how politics affects not only both one's living order and world order, but one's personal relationship as well. In this chapter my hope was to describe the people behind the politics.

Politics, through the ages and especially in current times, has certainly gained an increasingly negative vibration. Whether it's politics in the work place, a country's government, within a relationship (infidelity is bred on low self-esteem — why is that?), or within a family — politics has made life very uncomfortable; yet, it's needed to keep relations and orders stable.

Would it not be nice if all lived like those early Aztecs and Spaniards, whose government only had to worry about themselves? They had to keep order within their own people with much less care of the outside — until bored and wanting more thus allowing the Dark Side to enter.

These days, the world has become so small because it's so easy to connect with, and depend on country-to-country relationships, that there is a much higher need for a unified World Order — more on this in Chapter 7. The Dark Triad is growing. We need the Light Triad to prevail for a peaceful life.

From the 1999 Stephen King movie, *The Green Mile*, with Tom Hanks as Warden Paul Edgecomb and Michael Clarke as John Coffey, who was on death row for apparent murder:
"I'm tired, boss. Mostly I'm tired of people being so ugly to each other."
John Coffey

Chapter 5

The Power of Numbers: Mob/Herd Mentality

"A lie doesn't become truth, wrong doesn't become right and evil doesn't become good, just because it's accepted by a majority."
Author unknown

What side of politics are you on: right side or left side; or does it matter? More importantly, however, what side of life, your Living Order, do you live from? Do you even know or care about what your actions portray to others about your views? How about your partner? Is he or she honestly on a side that is constructive to yours, or is it potentially destructive? I ask again, does it matter?

Remember in Chapter 4, I said, "to matter" or "to have meaning" is something every living creature, at least us humans, want.

Being part of something is very cool. Being with one person, or a group of people, be it family or friends, our "tribe" (group of like-minded people) that bring to us the feeling that we "matter" — all are extremely healthy for every part of us humans. Animals feel it as well. It's paramount to sustaining our own good self-esteem! But then there's also "feeling good" based on social media (stay tuned for Chapter 11).

From the 1996 movie *Independence Day* starring Jeff Goldblum as David and Margaret Colin as ex-wife Constance, when David is feeling defeated due to his failed marriage and the eminent alien attack:

Constance: "David, haven't you ever wanted to be part of something special?"

David: "I was part of something special!"

Question for you (and this is a HUGE question and realization on your part): what is causing that "feeling" you have in order to "matter"?

To revisit the end of Chapter 3 and add to that quote from Jack Nicholson, regarding, "You can't handle the truth!" Are you afraid of your truth and can you face it?

I am repeating quite a few key phrases as they are important in order to understand one's "self." Humans thrive on the need to feel good about something — to celebrate. We certainly have different ways of showing it, but our minds desire the energy it can give. This may be shown best by how we celebrate the New Year coming in. Whatever culture, religion, and social level of living you are connected to, we celebrate the New Year, even when the date of the New Year differs with culture. Sports is another forum we love to show celebration, be it the Olympics, our country's team, our city's team, our school team and especially one's individual win.

Sports, professional and Olympic sports, and yes, even New Year's (although we will stay with sports here), is the ultimate equalizer to quash/suppress, for at least a moment, the dark side of a mob/herd mentality, and especially racism.

Professional sports are about representing a specific Living Order: a city, province, state, country, hemisphere, etc... When the team is competing and trying to win for that living order, all within the order are on the same side when the game is on and they are in the moment of competing.

Regardless of the player's colour, the players and the fans view the team's, or individual's, ethnicity as the same, which they believe in and so they root and cheer them on, forgetting all judgements.

Some of the athletes I noted in Chapter 3 such as Michael Jordan and Tiger Woods, have been, and remain my idols. however, if I remarry, they will likely not be invited to attend my wedding. I can handle only so much hypocrisy.

Both Michael and Tiger are black, African-American, and reached being the best at their respective professional sports, I have never heard reports saying "anyone" has made a racist statement towards them, especially when they were being the "athlete" that they became. They carried a charisma that was, and still is, hypnotic even to the worse of people, it seems. I'd be naïve and ignorant to assume that they have never faced racist comments and actions, but when they performed, regardless of their colour, all sports fans "seemed" good with them. This is the way it must always be, with everyone, no matter where they come from or what they look like!

Serena Williams however, the African-American female tennis start who also reached the best at her sport, has had to deal not only with racism, but also being female. This too must change! Neither should ever be an issue for judgement.

Even American Olympian, runner Jesse Owens, at the 1936 Olympics in Berlin, Germany, in front of the watching Adolf Hitler, won four gold medals and set three world records — all under the pressures of Hitler's Aryan/white supremacist theory. Here was a black man, an African-American, competing for the United States in the most high profile of activities, in the home of and in front of a tyrant who would soon try to take over the world — and sports, in particular one man, conquered all for the moment.

Whether you are a fan of sports or not, the psychological metamorphosis of fans rooting for their team at game time, regardless of differences, is truly something to acknowledge, admire, and find ways to sustain and expand outside of sports. "This" is why we need sports and what the Olympics are all about!

We cheer with everyone else. It's usually a very healthy and fun thing. It only changes from fun to dangerous when you get one or more people who feel they "need" to make a physical statement on how wrong everyone else is, or, they need to feel big themselves due to how little and inferior they feel.

European football/soccer has had some famous clashes where fights have broken out in the stands: two countries competing against each other and the competition has gone into the stands with mostly men taking patriotism too far. People have died in the stands. There have been stampedes. The stadiums have collapsed due to the mob fighting. This is happening in the current times of the 2020s. Ironically, there is little fighting among the actual competitive players.

Now, North American hockey, in particular professional/NHL levels, had its share of fighting amongst the players and the crowds watching.

The NHL, for their credit, has come along way in curbing the fighting on ice between the players. Fighting is still accepted, for some reason I personally don't buy into, but it has decreased — in particular the all-out bench brawls where entire teams would flood the ice with rock-em-sock-em robot-style fighting. The crowds cheered! Back then were the days of the Roman Gladiators. The fans were yelling, "Kill him, kill him!" I mean the hockey fans of recent times were yelling that!! At least the Roman crowds had a chance to give "thumbs up" or "thumbs down" to the fate of the defeated.

These same actions, depicted above, during an NHL hockey fight are sadly even intense during a university/college or even a house-league level hockey game. Get the parents of the players agitated, and ironically some of the most embarrassingly juvenile behaviour takes place in the stands. The players do not

Human Mechatronics™: The Double-Edged Power of Influence

fight but the parents erupt in name-calling, not only another parent but the player him/her self as well. Swearing and cheap verbal shots take place to try and bring their target's self-esteem down and hopefully affect their play in a negative way. Do you truly believe this is good role-modelling? Do you really believe this is your right — that this is your "freedom of speech" — to publicly and verbally fight with others, especially in front of your children, just for the sake of team support and need to show some power to feel empowered yourself? Is that a productive role model? What defines being all grown up and mature? What type of person do you want your young child to emulate when they get older?

All of the above started off with this feeling of familiarity, which leads to being "comfortable" with our "self." When we are in a place where we have that feeling of fitting in — where we feel we can connect and relate to others — and when we feel the others feel the same way as we do, then we are comfortable. The mind eases up on the fight vs. flight decision.

This "familiar" feeling, however, is where it can be dangerous. Is it familiar because of past experiences — a trigger to the subconscious part of your mind?

It could be something wonderful, a feeling of love, of fun, of feeling like you counted for something. Is it familiar due to something, maybe not even something you yourself have physically lived through? It could be something your mind has manifested into a subconscious reality. This is psychological scotoma. Is it familiar due to the level of energy you have been hoping to find: regardless of whether it's bad or good energy — it still increases your heartbeat and makes you excited. You just want to feel something, even if it's fear itself? Historical cult leaders such as Charles Manson, Jim Jones, Shoko Asahara and Marshall Applewhite knew how to smell that fear, befriend and manipulate people so much they would die for them.

If you have a clear and conscious mind, able to see all you

need to see, and think for yourself, then maybe it truly is a good familiarity and there's nothing to worry about.

However, when a preying and controlling person (again low self-esteem/narcissism) wants to "hook" you, they play to your needs, thinking they are your weaknesses. They go for your emotional centre. Once you say to yourself, "Wow, this person cares about me," you are then most vulnerable to be exactly that: "hooked!" They have found an opening in your mental door to manipulating you.

How can you tell? Stressing the point — this is a person with low self-esteem (they do not feel good about themselves!) and they will use that opening to try and control you — to bring your self-esteem down so they can feel they are better than you. This is false and mentally fabricated to appease their own beliefs. The charm excites you, but make no mistake, it can be very powerful and debilitating to you. They get so good at hiding it so you can't see it. They will probably make you feel over-the-moon about yourself, at an extreme level, which to you of course feels good. Meet the "Bully," the bully full of charisma.

Bullies: the louder they are, the more they talk and pick on/accuse others, the more they are protecting against fears they have about themselves, and they are there — deep inside, buried through hypnotic or retrograde amnesia. To get their way, bullies force themselves to live in the dark side — the Dark Triad. They are good at portraying themselves as supreme alphas, and need to recruit enough weak betas who feed them the energy to constantly add fuel to their fire, for it is in reality very weak. They show their strength through power over others.

Mob mentality stems from all the above in this chapter. On a lighter side, the expression "jumping on the bandwagon" also means joining a group "mindset." Mob mentality, though, is usually characterized as negative, hurtful, and damaging attitudes that are combined with physical actions taking place and manifesting within a group format.

Human Mechatronics™: The Double-Edged Power of Influence

It usually starts with one person, maybe narcissistic, maybe not, but certainly a charismatic individual with enough charm and voice in order to persuade and convince others to buy into their thinking. All he or she needs to find is one or two others thinking the same to feed that initial fire, then the snowballing effect happens, and increases the base of "believers." Does this also sound like the start of a cult? Sure it does! The idea is to form a "team," "group," "tribe," "following" of same-faith believers who want to protest something they don't like, all led by an authoritarian figure who has succumbed to their obsessive and contagious dark power.

What is it that causes usually young, seemingly very intelligent men and women to let down all their guards and be brainwashed into turning into someone totally different than who they were?

That desperate need to "matter" along with "fitting in with others," led by someone who sees that incredible vulnerability, and has the intelligence and charisma themselves to influence, is exactly how masses, mobs and most definitely cults are formed.

Private and usually secret (at least at the core of the control) mass "groups" or "secret societies" such as Heaven's Gate, The Spiritual Warrior Journey, and the Mankind Project have been led by extremely brilliant Machiavellian individuals, the likes of: Charles Manson, James Ray, and Jim Jones, of the Jonestown massacre in Guyana where 900 people drank a deadly-designed koolaid concoction being influenced and convinced to take their own lives under the direction of their cult leader. There is Japanese dance master and Buddhist, Terugoshi Kotoura, a.ka. "Katsura Kan" who established his macabre butoh dance class at the Buddhist private Naropa University in Boulder, Colorado, and who in 2012 had taken control of and married a young, beautiful, and very intelligent Sharon Stern from an affluent family. Kotoura's manipulation reached an apex when Stern was so deeply into depression that she took her own life. Since then her parents have set up the *Families Against Cult Teachings* along with numerous lawsuits against Kan.

Names of other people, mostly young women, as sadly history is flooded with the need of men to prove and demonstrate their perceived positive self-esteem through power over women, include Patty Hearst and actress Allison Mack from the television series, *Smallville*, who became a prominent leader, and whom with leader Keith Raniere's a.k.a. "Vanguard" sex cult group, Nxivm, was charged in 2019 with conspiracy and extortion, sex-trafficking and racketeering when the cult was exposed.

What happens, then, when an event of major proportions such as a major earthquake or sudden governmental collapse happens, and masses of people come out to the street and all hell breaks loose with pandemonium? Individuals become looters, breaking into stores to steal whatever they can get their hands on, usually starting with alcohol and big-ticket items such as stereo and television equipment. Men chase and gang-rape defenceless females and beat-up on singled-out males.

Sadly, the people who jump on "that' kind of bandwagon are severe extremists. This type of behaviour is often driven by such a low sense of self-esteem — similar to the quote noted in the Preface about Ringo from the movie *Tombstone*; he or she is internally angry at their own "being" that they need to look at controlling others to make them happy. They need to inflict pain, mentally and/or physically, and they feel this intense sense of entitlement as a form of not only retribution for the life they live, but also as reconciliation.

Here is where we revisit why I decided to make two books out of one. In the Introduction, I noted the current status, mostly in the United States, due to the death of George Floyd, an African American who died under the knee of a Minnesota police officer.

Human Mechatronics™: The Double-Edged Power of Influence

Today, June 1, 2020, the U.S.A., parts of Canada, and the world have been under major protest, and even to the level of rioting, over the injustice felt by not only the black world, but all coloured cultures, be they white or brown, etc… I struggle to even use these terms to define any one culture. Colour should not matter. Defining and judging based on colour is what racism is all about, over and above the treatment of the same.

George Floyd (R.I.P.) was shown on live video as being a human being who may have made a mistake, but ended up being attacked, and died while being controlled by the very person who was sworn to protect the human race. There was never a threat of life shown against the police officers.

We need the police. We need protection. But with any living order, and the police force is one, there are people who abuse the system. That is what happened here; not just one police officer, but four white officers in total abused the system against a defenceless and unarmed black man, regardless of his past.

Mr. Floyd was not the first. The world is tired of the injustice against the black society. Back in Chapter 3, I noted football quarterback Colin Kaepernick taking a knee at a football game as a protest to the injustice. Today we have rioting going on for the same reason: social injustice against black Americans. The world is tired of xenophobic people. The world is tired of racism.

The stories are there. With Mr. Floyd, you can find it all over YouTube, social and network media and so on, so I am not going to describe the graphics here again. Going by the roughly nine-minute video alone, this was a gross miscarriage of police power. The way George Floyd was treated, who is heard begging for his life, was a grotesque and atrocious death.

That is as far as I go taking sides. I do not know George Floyd. I know nothing about him or his past. I only open up minds to become creative free, albeit civilized and caring thinkers.

What was caught on video, showing his graphic death, is what has triggered the people's fire! No one should ever die that way, in public or in private: my opinion — yes.

Now let's talk about mob mentality as it relates to the George Floyd death. We all should have a right to express, in a constructive way, our disgust, our anger, and our rage. This time it is over what has happened in this moment, and time and time again in society due to the colour of one's skin: racism. We are sick and tired of being sick and tired with prejudice, abuse of power, mistrust and, yes, racism of any type and from all sides.

> To quote from a song by Aerosmith
> "If you can judge a wise man, by the colour of his skin,
> Then mister you're a better man that I"
> *Living On The Edge*: Aerosmith

So YES, protest, march, raise your voice, and lift your signs! There are times when reform must happen and this IS one of those times. Do it out of anger, however, not hatred and violence! Bring hatred into the equation, and you feed fuel to the dark side of immorality. In a mob situation, this is where it gets out of hand with dark people trying to influence a peaceful demonstration into becoming a riot, full of looting, destruction, buildings and vehicles on fire, injuries and even deaths among the protesters themselves. This has all happened throughout at least forty states in the 7-day (to the point where I am typing this) aftermath of George Floyd's murder.

Even today, Mr. Floyd's family has appealed publicly to the protesters to keep it peaceful. Nobody else needs die. Today, numerous police in multiple cities, are honouring George Floyd by taking a knee, as Colin Kaepernick did, with the protestors in the streets, to show solidarity with the very people they are trying to maintain order with. See, there is good in people.

At this moment of final editing, I am adding the following: It is June 7, 2020, and I think, the 12th day of world protesting against what happened to Mr. Floyd which, all became about

Human Mechatronics™: The Double-Edged Power of Influence

racism, social injustice, police brutality and federal politics. We have had riots: cities being partly destroyed with fires, looters having destroyed small family-run businesses, and people and police officers have been severely injured — even killed. The American President has threatened Nation-wide curfews and even martial law over and above State Governors. Thousands of troops via martial law has been deployed in Washington D.C., in front of the White House, to fight peace by using force to take control for a Presidential photo-op at a church.

Both edges of power via the people have come clashing together juxtaposed over top and while clashing on top of both edges of power from the accepted enforcers and decision-makers a.k.a. government who are clashing between themselves. Read that again because I know how confusing in seems. I don't know how else to describe it.

"A riot is the language of the unheard"
Martin Luther King Jr.

And, this is all the while the world is "trying" to open up while still mostly being in quarantine due to the Covid19 virus pandemic. Kudos to the protesters as in every city, in every country I have seen displayed on news network, while social distancing has been thrown out the window, it seems a good majority of all ages are wearing masks! Good for you people!

It is an unprecedented period of real-time world history being created right before our eyes, especially with the news and social media coverage bringing the public right to the frontline of the demonstrations.

What you just read must sound like total chaos and anarchy. It has been just that. Yet, this very day, even while tens-of-thousands are still strong in city streets — the adrenaline, the rage, the thirst for vengeance has calmed somewhat with riots subsiding as level heads start prevailing and charges have been laid in George Floyd's death. Even past deaths of black men and women under the control of police, have had their cases be reopened. The NFL has even publicly apologized for how it handled the protest of Colin Kaepernick although, they never mentioned Colin's name and no action has yet to take place to rectify his banishment from the sport.

Washington D.C. Mayor Muriel Browser has the two-block-long section of street just up from the White House, be renamed as Black Lives Matter Plaza complete with 35-foot high (11m) yellow capital letters painted on 16th Street NW in downtown Washington. I make no judgement on this. This action is deemed as positive action for the cause behind the protesting. The naysayers will spin it any other way they wish.

The world is speaking and though it's not easy, it's not without pushback — some of the right people are hearing the pain and have started to take positive action. The world wants peace and harmony, and accountability for those who are not with that program.

I urge you all to rent out the powerful 2000 movie, *Remember The Titans* starring Denzel Washington for how the moviemakers can create a beautiful and true story based on races coming together as one. It is the best movie I know of for these times we currently in. It is a football movie but it is not about football. It is about racism, sexism, homosexuality, power, fear, politics, hypocrisy, politics, religion, war, hate and, most of all, love. It shows how adversity can be conquered. It shows how differences can be embraced instead of judged. It shows how respect can lead to incredible power.

Please then watch the award-winning, 1998 television film entitled *Ruby Bridges*. Based on the true story of Ruby Bridges who, in 1960, as a six-year-old black first-grader, became the first black student in the all-white William Frantz Public School in New Orleans, Louisiana. Talk about pressure and fear; she came to school that morning of Monday, November 14, 1960 guided by her mother, and federal marshals who would continue to escort her to school through the year. How's that for overcoming negative influence? How's that for the bravery of a six-year-old child whose history is about slavery and hate, to find the inner courage and focus needed to better herself so she can better this world? Ruby Bridges is still alive today in 2020.

As a protester, as part of a pack, a mob, a herd, you run with a crowd; however, when it comes to rioting, it has been manipulated to show hatred, and you enter the dark side, and end up running with the bulls causing massive destruction. You have now become counterproductive and hypocritical to the very people you are advocating for.

Yet, you want to be heard. If you are not heard and there is no reform after trying, and trying, and after repeated deaths — then sadly, things will escalate.

You! You have a choice to make when subjected to this kind of culture. We've talked about the fight vs. flight but now we are introduced to a third choice: to join!

To fight a group, let alone a mob, as an individual, is dangerous and may even end in your own tragedy of some-sort. This leaves you to run and stay safe, or join. It depends on the nature of the beast; the reason the mob was created. There are many good reasons for group behaviour that are backed by positive and respectful principles and morals. We need to survive, and sometimes we need the help of the masses. Sometimes, we need the voices.

That is your choice. That is your own: recognition of the event, defining what is happening, your analysis of good or bad for you, and your measuring of danger vs. excitement and thus, your involvement.

Is it confusing? Damn right it's confusing! The mind can only take so much then it becomes what's known as "Cognitive

Dissonance." Taken from Google it means: "the state of having inconsistent thoughts, beliefs, or attitudes, especially as relating to behavioural decisions and attitude changes."

Now it is up to you and your six characteristic traits: Wisdom, Imagination, Memory, Will, Intuition, and Reasoning, in order to limit what is entering your conscious mind through the five senses. Your limbic system has triggered "fight or flight." This will all come together in Part 2: *Human Mechatronics*™.

Chapter 6

Hate vs. Love:
Why We Are Alive: Gratitude

What if Hernan Cortez and his band of Spaniards had not decided to take over the Aztec Empire? Where would we be today? Would we have the life we have today?

What if, after World War I, Britain and France had not imposed the Treaty of Versailles on Germany with financial penalties and sanctions sending them into an economic crisis and a falling of their Empire?

Then, what if, in World War II, Germany had not been so pissed off and try to take over parts of Europe? What if the U.S. had not dropped the bomb on Hiroshima, Japan? What if Canada, along with the other allied countries, had not been instrumental in attacking the beaches of France in June of 1944?

Each of these examples, these events, these actions, were built on anger and hate, and love. Ironic, isn't it? Anger and hate for what a country has suffered through, regardless of who and how it started yet, but each country does what they do out of the love for their own. Each country engages in a mob mentality approach to protect and defend itself, and/or to drive ahead with what they, the government, believe in.

So much bloodshed was spilled. So many humans, in the millions, if not billions, have died for those causes.

Living where and how I live today, in Ontario, Canada — secure, free, as safe as I could hope for — it would be all too easy for me to say I wish those events had never happened. I feel that would be very naïve and disrespectful of me. I did not live through those times to understand the desperation, fear, and anger people must have felt.

I have no problem in saying I am sad that people had to die in order to defend their countries. Sure, some cultures say, "To die in battle, that is to die with honour!" To me, for anyone to die is tragic, but especially when it's because you are trying to protect yourself and others, along with the security and safety of your living order.

Which comes first: human survival or nation (country) survival? Can one be without the other? It is possible to survive as a human alone - without a nation. It is not possible for a nation to survive without its humans?

So, all this killing and bloodshed, and hate — that was all good? Seriously!? If so, why isn't it good today? But wait, these days, in "civilized" countries, it seems that maybe lessons have been learned. Some countries have also grown so powerful on a world scale, and in their own right, that no country dares challenge them. Oh, they may threaten in order to show their supposed strength, even if in glancing blows, but nothing will ever happen due to the catastrophic cost. Or will it?

On the flipside, there are still cultures, countries and, yes, governments that are still very much old school and need to constantly plan for the threat of attack, domination and war.

If people learned to respect and be grateful for where they are right now; right this moment within the world, they would realize that world domination is only fun playing the game of Risk with friends and drinks.

There are many, millions, who do not live as fortunate as I do. I wish they all could. That in alone is part of what immigration is about. People want to leave their backward living orders. They want to leave their repressed and controlling

Human Mechatronics™: The Double-Edged Power of Influence

countries in order to have a better chance at living a life that counts.

Why does that seems to mean though, that, while being an open nation to completely different world orders, that our institutions, our practices, our heritage and rituals, become offensive to the very people we welcome in, so much so, that we are the ones who change in order to make it "nice" and "peaceful."

Indigenous people occupied the early lands. They had little power over the evolving masses of evolution and sadly was a period of much bloodshed. In today's current fight against social and racial injustice however, the indigenous are receiving at least some respect for who and what they represent.

The mosaic of many countries such as my homeland, Canada were then built and thrived on immigration. They need to continue to do so, yet current day immigration takes two of those original life basics, faith and religion, to the point where natives now are afraid to say, "Merry Christmas," or read the bible in schools. It is said we change like this out of respect for the beliefs of those joining our country. Respect however, starts with being grateful by acknowledging and appreciating the culture of those who are giving others a renewed lease on life.

I believe, speaking from living in a country like Canada, that most are grateful for what we have. I believe that most of us agree to allowing complete strangers, many who come from war-torn societies much like some of our own ancestors, to enter into our country. Without control and regulations however, it can lead to chaos, meltdown of an established order, and possibly even war — especially a cold civil war which, presently in some other nations, may very well be on the verge of evolving.

Marcus Aurelius speaks to Maximus, his saviour and second father, played by Russell Crowe, in the 2000 David Franzoni movie, *Gladiator*.

Marcus Aurelius: " I have been at war. I know what's out there."

From another scene in *Gladiator* —I'm sure that there are some nations that today, in 2020, pray for the following to happen:

Marcus Aurelius: "I want you to become the protector of Rome after I die. I will empower you to one end alone: to give power back to the people of Rome, and end the corruption that has crippled it. Will you accept this great honour I have offered you?"
Maximus: "With all my heart, no."
Marcus Aurelius: "Maximus, that is why it must be you."
Maximus: "But surely a prefect, a senator, somebody who knows the city, who understands politics?"
Marcus Aurelius: "But you have not been corrupted by her politics."

And still one more scene from *Gladiator,* involving Proximo who helped Maximus as a slave:

Proximo: "I wasn't the best because I killed quickly. I was the best because the crowd loved me. Win the crowd and you'll win your freedom."
Maximus: "I will win the crowd. I will give them something they have never seen before."

Doesn't this sound very familiar to what certain nations today are living through politically? Some leaders win the crowd "only" because they know how to influence and manipulate the weak-minded hiding behind low self-esteem.

I did not initially like the movie, *Gladiator*. As I allowed my mind to open up and not be so objective to the violence alone, it became a favourite via the study of these hate vs. love and self-esteem portrayals.

I am truly grateful for the life I have. I know I am one of the fortunate ones, as are my children, my friends, and my fellow Canadians.

I am alive because of what people — my parents and others — did; they jumped on the bandwagon out of fear and anger in order to protect what we have here in Canada. Here there were two levels of fear, and it was the fight or flight question: "Do we stay and be controlled, or leave to find ourselves and our own life?" Once that is decided, there is only one thing to do: join.

Fear: "Does not kill you but prevents you from living."

Paradox: the meaning, taken from Wikipedia, is "a seemingly absurd or self-contradictory statement or proposition that when investigated or explained may prove to be founded or true."

From the movie: *The Two Towers (The Lord of the Rings)* by J.R.R. Tolkien:
"War must be, while we defend our lives against a destroyer who would devour all; but I do not love the bright sword for its sharpness, nor the arrow for its swiftness, nor the warrior for his glory. I love only that which they defend."

Life, and the world we live in, is such a paradox. Absurd things happen all the time, yet sometimes it makes sense, or at least we form a level of scotoma that rationalizes the logic of it happening.

We must never forget the words of Joshua a.k.a. the NATO computer called WOPR from the 1983 movie, *War Games*, starring Ally Sheedy and Matthew Broderick. Joshua is talking to his creator Dr. Stephen Falken, played by John Woods, after the computer is led into playing a specific game of hopeful education in the final seconds prior to the suspenseful launch code start of a thermonuclear war it initiated:

Joshua: "Greeting Professor Falken."

Prof. Falken: "Hello Joshua."
Joshua: "Strange game. The only winning move is not to play. How about a nice game of ?" (not going to spoil the movie ending ;-)

Chapter 7

The World Order

Finally, after all my mentioning, let's look at what the "World Order" is all about.

The definition, taken from the Oxford dictionary via Google is: "a system controlling events in the world, especially a set of arrangements established internationally for preserving global political stability."

I like to think of world order as gravity. Gravity is the reason the earth remains in its position within the solar system. Gravity is what keeps the solar system itself in order with the galaxy and the universe. This is the universal order. If one of the planets were to come out of their place within that order, it could have catastrophic consequences on the survival of all remaining planets.

Once the aggregate mixture of each and every individual part is thrown together and mixed, the end result is an agreed upon consistent system based on the aggregate working together within the system to give the desired end product. That is how we bake cookies and that is how we nations work with each other.

When my marital and post-marital family was together, I was the baker. I was also the balancer, taking each and every member of the family — their strengths, their talent, their mindset, their dislikes, anything that make up who they were — helping build their aptitude by guiding them to make it all work together for the best possible outcome within the living order they will choose.

When we find a balance, can things change? Can one or more items be added? Absolutely, yes! Quadrantic Cognition™ will talk about that more in Book 2. That is what evolution and growth is about — growing and changing, changing and growing, sometimes with clear vision and focus; sometimes by trial and error. However, whether a two-person relationship, a family, a church, a school, a village, city, province or state, and even a country — the changes have to somehow still balance out within the system, or the system becomes unstable, with many potential problems.

As noted in the previous chapter, there is so much diversity in this world we call Earth — so many different cultures, and mindsets, religions, beliefs about how we came to existence. I could go on and on. They do not all agree with each other. A high majority of the diversity however, has learned to respect and work together. And, that is a great thing! It's called being diplomatic. Here we go again with politics. See — you can't avoid it no matter where you hide. J

When negotiations get played out many times like a game of chess, usually through government and hard politics, establishing one's agreed upon position yet six moves later the one country knows it will all change — ideally to their benefit — eventually some countries come to terms on an agreement.

NATO: North Atlantic Treaty Organization was created as an intergovernmental military alliance between 29 North American and European countries. NATO is who tracks the path of Santa Claus each year seeing he must visit each and every country J.

There's the in-the-moment changing NAFTA: North American Free Trade Agreement signed between Canada, the U.S.A and Mexico to deal with free trade in North America.

The EU: The European Union, which part of Britain so desperately wants to pull away from and be free on their own

Human Mechatronics™: The Double-Edged Power of Influence

via Brexit.

The G8: The Group of Eight, which now the removal of Russia for unfair practices: became the G7 much to the chagrin of one President whose self-proclaimed friend is Russia's communist dictator.

These are all multi-national organizations, that over time and as a result of deep and confrontational negotiations, came to be, as they worked towards a common goal — establishing a form of guidelines and rules for countries to abide by and make a new World Order that is sustainable and fair to all involved.

World economics is far too big a topic for this book. That is what school is for. What is important to note here is that most of these countries help each other out during turbulent times. Financially, each country relies on another for money, even in good times. World debt has gone crazy stupid. Even the United States, for all its power and wealth and job creation, owes all that currently because it has reached record levels of debt while it has had to decrease interest rates to sustain the economy with low inflation. Where do you think they get the money to decrease the deficit? The deficit the States bears could crush the country if there was another power big enough to take it to task and call it in or, if there were changes significant enough within the World Order to cause global economics to take revenge. We are so close to that very exact event happening, it is tragically scary. I say tragic because decades of financial abuse did not have to happen, if only governments had been honest and truly cared.

The world is so simple yet complex. There must be a world order that countries abide by. Ideally all countries buy into the same order but that is just a pipe dream. There are still too many individual countries with their own mindset that they believe to be the right one, contrary to all other nations' mindsets. The bloodshed and death still is prevalent regardless of how far some cultures have progressed.

Today, in 2020, there is a very fine line, which wavers every now and then, that stabilizes the balance and we all mostly stay at peace.

For the most part, there is thankfully a respect countries have for each other that is abided by. Iraq can co-exist with Iran. North Korea can co-exist with South Korea. They do not destroy each other, but every now and then there is destruction and death to remind all that friction still exists.

Russia and Ukraine? The old mindset of control and takeover unfortunately still exists with both Russia's current invasion of its neighbour, Ukraine, and their welcome involvement with the United States.

The world order can certainly change with fluctuation in the plethora of living orders there are. This is immigration. Living orders merge with other living orders. It can be done with grace and ease; however, if personalities cause a clash among the characteristics of those set orders — that is where conflict can arise.

Chapter 8

The Living Order™

So many times through this book I have mentioned the "Living Order." Now that we have an understanding of the global "World Order" and why it is what it is, let us look at the "Living Order": the social make-up and influence of your immediate day-to-day life and where you live.

I could not find a definition anywhere, so I am going to create one modifying the same World Order definition taken from the Oxford dictionary via Google. The Living Order is: "a system controlling events in the more immediate culture in which you live in, especially a set of arrangements established for preserving immediate cultural stability."

Culture, taken from the Oxford dictionary via Google, is: "The customs, arts, social institutions, and achievements of a particular nation, people, or other social group."

The Living Order exists within a family, a school, a business, a sports team, and an association of individuals supporting any given cause. Living order is the way of behaviour for all those involved — a code of conduct.

You are born into a living order. In your early years you had no choice, you were taken care of (well or maybe not so well) by that living order, which was usually, but not always, your family. That can change depending on numerous things, including politics and/or religion and where you live within the world order.

In many religious families including both Christian and Catholic, if a child is sick, he or she is taken to a doctor for treatment. With some other religions/faiths, the parents do not believe in medicinal healing and deny their child medical treatment. This has been challenged in court many times. The child becomes the victim here when an accepted living order is being selfishly superseded by an arrogant and self-satisfying belief. Many children have suffered and died because of this exact situation.

Once on our own, we choose the life we want to live. It has been heavily influenced but it remains our choice to be who we are. If you are to find comfort within, you develop appreciative thinking and, for the most part, accept your living order.

You answered the questions at the beginning of the book regarding, "Who are you?" Here's a new question. What defines you?"

Is it your job? Is it your bank account? Is it your house, your car, the size of land you own — maybe that you have a swimming pool? Do you live with a maximalistic philosophy meaning more is more which, you perceive to define your power (remember we talked at the beginning of this book about "status" being an artificial level of power)? Is it how many friends you have and how popular you are? Is it the quantity and the size of rings that are on your fingers — tattoos and piercings on your body? Is it the labels on your purse, or shoes, or who made your clothes? Is it the power you feel being in a gang? Is it a gun you own or how loud your voice can get? Are you defined by what flag you fly? Did you bring your personal living order from somewhere else in the world order, trying to integrate it within your new living order without any social care or respect for the established? Yes, this was an attempt at being diplomatic about misused immigration. Is it your cell phone and how you think you may appear so busy all the time and thus successful to others? Is it your ability to voice your opinion as an armchair quarterback on social media — enough to get attention where one's possible malevolent nature tries to influence the narrative with nasty and vulgar comments regarding what others post? One's low self-esteem has found a faceless avenue of attack for the sad zealot. Is it how well you score on dating sites? Is it why some believe they can always find a better partner through the Internet? Is it how many beautiful women you have in your friend list or the controlling bad-boy males you must have connection with to feel secure?

Does your relationship define you: how your partner looks to you and possibly for you, how others view your partner as a reflection of you?

Or, are you defined by how you feel you fit within your living order? Is it a feeling of peace with the people that surround you? Maybe it's a feeling of unease or awkwardness within the same. Whether good or not so good, I'm just trying to help you think about your answer. Is it how you feel you are part, or not a part of your neighbourhood, your classmates, your social groups, and your job culture? Is it how you have worked hard, or maybe not so hard, at achieving your goals such as being an athlete, taking care of your body/machine, a musician, a writer, a volunteer, or a helper to your cultural causes? Is it how you can feel the positive energy from the love people express to you for who you are and what you do to help make your living order behave within that mutual code of conduct?

The first list described material things that some humans feel they need to have or achieve in order to feel good about themselves. They are highly based on how we hope "others" admire our "self."

The second list described mostly things that were more personal and of emotion, and therefore of our mind. They were about things "you yourself" felt about your "self."

True power within a living order is of the mind — it is not

artificial based on possessions and status.

Individuals do not all agree amongst their tribe. Unless you are living in a dictatorship, a state-run country or the like — in a democratic government, you the people have a voice, as an individual and as a collective. Even if it's not democratic, you can still hopefully speak, shout, jump up and down, and protest with a specific cause, and without further violence.

In our individual lives, if there is that Living Order where we can find peace, freedom, opportunity, familiarity, meaning and have a chance to matter — then we need to be grateful for that and work with that order.

There will always be differences. There will always be independent views and forced perceptions. Without a strong and clear mind, people will believe what they want to believe regardless of hard, concrete facts: remember psychological scotoma. People will struggle to find focus and sometimes they will focus on something they have "allowed" themselves be brainwashed into thinking is right.

Chapter 9

MeFirst – When Things Work Out – Temptation – Fame

Picture yourself driving on a congested four-lane road, approaching the on-ramp to the freeway. You are the lead car of five vehicles. Suddenly, as you are about to merge into the on-ramp, a car in the left lane speeds past you and cuts sharply across in front of you. The driver of that car is now first in line with no one to hold him or her back. Sound familiar?

You and the others have been patient and respectful of everyone else who is part of this congestion, or order. You all know it takes time. I know what's going through your mind — the driver has no respect for living order here and how you and others have worked as a group.

That driver, to be first, ahead of everyone else, had to make the conscious choice to be selfish, act aggressively, and drive dangerously. There were a lot of assumptions that driver made. What if you had sped up suddenly, thinking about the fact you are getting on a freeway? A collision would have been a near certainty. This attitude is a reflection of much of today's society.

We live in a MeFirst society today more than ever before. It has become such a material world at such a high level. People feel they are entitled to so much at such an early stage. And while we all, myself included, want to feel success and enjoy its rewards as early as possible, gone are the lessons learned when one pays their dues by starting small and evolving through trial and error. Graduating from school today means an expected $70,000/yr career — immediately!

Just as the young generation does today, thirty or forty years ago many of us also went to university and college. We came out of there with huge debts and many of us started from scratch at jobs that were not even close to what we went to school for. I don't wish that on anyone because, yes, it is hard and frustrating.

What's sad and scary today is that the government wants you to feel this exact way. They want you to feel that entitlement. By doing so you will spend your money. The banks, driven by the government — or is it visa versa — keep the interest rates low in order to make it easy for you to buy with credit. Enter marketing and advertising and cognitive manipulation. That's not the only reason of course, but it is one of many.

Through this social media on the internet, and even television, there is a new level of propaganda attempting to entice the young generations to buy more on credit. The financial sector smells the entitlement the young feel. Advertisements for credit companies such as: *Credit Karma*, *Credit Sesame*, and *Experian*. These are consumer credit companies whose commercials are ridiculously insulting to one's intelligence in that they make getting credit so easy yet do nothing to educate the downfalls of living in credit. Also ridiculous is the notion that you can "make money" by getting cash back, the more you spend. Duh!! Remember what the word "gullible" means! Just as the tobacco companies having to list the dangers of smoking on cigarette packages, the same needs to be done when applying for credit. I know far too many people, including myself, who have struggled because we did not appreciate the dangers of taking on credit.

Remember, the money we borrow from the bank is borrowed from the government, which is borrowed from other countries. Not only are countries in debt-crisis mode; individual debt is at an all-time high. Young couples are carrying mortgages of $300,000+ for homes they feel they need to own. These are unprecedented debts. All it takes is for the world order to get off balance, and then our living order will certainly be thrown off balance as well. But, that's okay, right, because when things work out, one feels the entitlement to have it all?

In the 1980s, the interest rates went to twenty-one percent due to a world economics crisis over oil. People lost their homes, had to increase their mortgages at twenty-one percent in order to try and stay afloat, and many people took their own lives because of the inability to financially survive.

Wanting more – wanting it all – wanting fame. In this book, many movies are being referenced. What would we do without movies — without Hollywood and Bollywood? What would we do without the entertainment of the movies and other arts?

These exist because of supply and demand. Someone puts out something new, people like it, they are willing to pay money for it, to see more of it, and boom — you have an industry. In the case of movies, music, writing, painting, even sports; the artists providing the entertainment get paid. Increase the demand and you increase what they get paid. Fair enough — makes sense, right? Along with that comes more fame for the artist. Can fame get to be too much?

History answers with a resounding, yes! There are scores of examples where, sadly, becoming famous has changed, or triggered something, in the mind of many stars and it has become all about them — almost to a level of narcissism. There have never been more references to Alpha-Males or especially Alpha-Females in order to justify "Mefirst" mindsets, and actions, as there are today. Narcissism and entitlement are running rampant, hand-in-hand with the MeFirst world.

Today is the age of youth replying with "WTF," "Whatever," "Just sayin'" and "No Worries" to end conversations they don't like because it appears to be a weakness to agree with or appreciate someone else. What do "Whatever" and "Just sayin'" imply? Seriously, whatever happened to "Thank you," "You are welcome," or, if that is too much, "You're welcome!"? It seems that gone are the days of etiquette, involving graceful and polite communication within society.

So, what about the famous? What about those who may have, or may not have had, talents where they were able to take to an ultimate level of winning — those people who have stood on a platform and thanked their sources for helping them get there. It's a wonderful feeling. Isn't that what part of the competitive nature in us humans is all about; working hard and trying to win one for ourselves? How can there be anything negative in that?

This is where religion sometimes re-enters. So many times I have listened to an acceptance speech, be it winning in sports or winning an Oscar, where this person has said, "and I thank god for getting me this victory!" No! Your god did NOT help you with this victory. If so, then why did your god not help your competitor? God, as we know, has no bias — no favouritism. Your god may have given you natural born talents, skills that YOU, and likely many others helped to harness and bring to an extreme level, but that's it. Go ahead and say, "I thank my god for giving me the strength to train hard." That statement is based on your faith and belief. Congratulations, but it was YOU that brought your victory to you.

But what about those people we the audience, perceive to have worked it all out, and that we idolize, glorify, put on pedestals, dream of and fantasize about in our beds? The following have all achieved a great level of stardom, which has brought them wealth and admiration for their talents and skills, yet each and every one of them has ended up struggling:

- In Hollywood, what happened to Lindsay Lohan? What happened to Amanda Bynes, Zac Efron, Cara Delevingne, Catherine Zeta-Jones, Harrision Ford, Jim Carrey, 28-year-old Heath Ledger, 31-year old Corey Montieth, 25-year old actress and X-Factor U.S. Finalist Simone Battle, and, of course, 63-year-old Robin Williams?

* The list is countless from Hollywood alone. In the music scene, what happened to Britney Spears, Eminem, 34-year-old Layne Staley of *Alice and Chains* and others, 52-year-old Chris Cornell of *Soundgarden* and others, 31-year-old Terry Kath of *Chicago*, 27-year-old Janis Joplin, 55-year-old Brad Delp of *Boston*, 28-year-old Avicii (Tim Bergling) from Sweden, 69-year-old Butch Trucks of *The Allman Brothers*, 27-year-old Kim Jonghyun from South Korea, 24-year-old Goo Hara of *KARA* also of Korea, 27-year-old Amy Winehouse, 25-year old twice married and mother of two Peaches Geldof who yes, was daughter of musician/frontman of the Irish band, *Boomtown Rats* (song-I Don't Like Mondays) and creator of *Live-Aid*, Bob Geldof, 48-year-old Whitney Houston, and then there's 27-year-old Kurt Cobain of *Nirvana*.

- The third level of the arts is where we find the painters. Painters include 37-year-old Vincent Van Gogh, 27-year-old American Jean-Michel Basquiat and of course Spanish painter — the famous Pablo Picasso.

- Rounding out with the fourth level are the authors, which include 59-year-old Virginia Woolf, 67-year-old Hunter Thompson, 61-year-old Ernest Hemingway, and 30-year-old Sylvia Plath.

- Renowned author J.K. Rowling created the Harry Potter Dementors — those flying, caped demon-like figures that sucked happiness and spirit from humans and wizards to help her deal with a specific personal struggle.

Judgement is not always negative. To the audience, these and other famous people at the same level of public exposure seemed to have it all. They had the talent, the fame, they had the money, they had scores of fans — therefore they must have had happiness. Such a sad and naïve judgement that is.

There are so many — young and old. Add to those lists people like 17-year-old transgender Leelah Alcorn, wrestler Michael Lee Alfonso (Mike Awesome), 23-year-old Canadian porn actress Mercedes Grabowski (August Ames), and 29-year-old American YouTuber Desmond Daniel Amofah (Etika).

All of these people in the aforementioned lists had two things in common: they all dealt with their own personal mental-health wellness and many were succumbed by their own internal demons — in one form or another. (Sources: Wikipedia, ESPN, Entertainment Tonight, People Magazine) The number of people to include in these lists is staggering. This was just a fraction of the reality. The other thing in common: any who had their age shown ended up taking their own life via suicide. Close your eyes — think about that for a few seconds.

"Winning has a price. And Leadership has a price."
Michael Jordan from *The Last Dance*

Many reached out for help. They showed great inner strength. Many went public in order to get help and help others. Many went in and out of depression numerous times throughout their lives. Many had tremendous focus — for a while.

Most found ways to hide their demons. Most turned to excessive use of alcohol or drugs. Most exhibited ambivert tendencies, meaning they have a balance of both introvert and extrovert features. In private they were quiet and to themselves; in public and especially when it was show time, they often needed to be over-the-top expressive. In private is where the mental struggle flourished.

Human Mechatronics™: The Double-Edged Power of Influence

Most had some type of confusion or conflict, or just higher pressure when they were young children. That pressure wasn't necessarily bad. It could have been deemed great and productive for maturing at the time and was assumed that they were able to handle it — the fame, the adulation, both then and in their future. We adults make such stupid assumptions at times!

If you are a parent, however, I would like you to read the previous paragraph again, and again, and again.

It is fun, exciting, adrenalin creating, self-realizing and addictive when, as a child, we find something that we are good at. That's the way it should be! Self-expression is supposed to be what childhood is all about. It is also a way we escape pain.

Also tough is likely peer pressure, the manipulation and control, with or without intent (as the child, how are we supposed to know?), and the bullying that goes with it all.

Bullying in person, face-to-face, is terrible. Cyber-bullying has to be absolute hell. It is devastatingly cruel and torturous because it reached the masses in a second with social media — more of this in Chapter 11.

It has to be really tough when one's childhood fun turns into that elite level, where one needs to trust others to help, but one also has to believe in themselves to such an extreme level — to an almost arrogant level. As Yoda from *Star Wars* said, "There is no try! Just Do!" This is also not a light-switch that one can just turn on and off. You have to believe it, to become it! As a young person who shows elite talent, success and driving hard to achieve the goal of perfection is drilled into the psyche. And whose goal is it anyway that is being driven: the 8-year-old daughter who loves to sing to the songs she loves, the 14-year-old son who seems a natural for playing a guitar, the 17-year-old who has made the starting line-up for their high school's basketball team, or is this more than a parental support goal? Is this actually all about it being the parent's personal goal being reached through one's children, which was created based on something from "the parent's" past?

As a child, to find emotional balance, they need help – not assumptions. As an adult, it is also extremely difficult to emotionally balance it all, now with money, a relationship, material desires and achievement factoring in. Those four added pressures — remember this for Quadrantic Cognition™ — can take our behaviour to an uncontrolled and multi-personality level. Yet, we as adults, and young adults — even teenagers these days — think we know what to use to stop our wandering thoughts.

What happens when one feels they have it all but wants more? What is "more" when they've achieved and acquired the only thing they really wanted to do? It may be a simple answer to many; to many it's where the spirit and mind get lost in those wandering thoughts.

A word I talk about in my seminars is "Praxis" which taken from Google means: "a process by which a theory, lesson, or skill is enacted, embodied, or realized." In other words, to reach Praxis means "you are walking the talk so confidently because you fully and consciously believe in yourself!" This is a great place to be, full of personal power created by achieving a high level of focus. There is no arrogance involved. It is believing in yourself for your "self."

This is how I have had to live in order to get to the point of writing this book, and my previous books. This is not about "me" being "first." I have had a high sense of consciousness and self-awareness while doing this. I have been cognizant of every action. While it has been overwhelming at times, it has not owned my soul or my mind.

When we believe it for ourselves so much that we have excelled to the highest level of "self" — what more is there? Praxis!

Human Mechatronics™: The Double-Edged Power of Influence

The "MeFirst" mindset is real. It is what today has become. Putting oneself first is a good thing. It can motivate and inspire us, until it rules our psyche and we then judge and tear down or demean those who we perceive to be ahead of or better than us.

Is that who you want to be? Is that who you want to support? Is that the world you want you and your children to live in?

As Jack Nicholson earlier screamed, "You can't handle the truth!"

"Art is a kind of innate drive that seizes a human and makes him its instrument. The artist is not a person endowed with free will who seeks his own ends, but one who will allow art to release its purpose through him."
Jungian Therapy by Carl Jung

Chapter 10

The Speed of Life Today

At the time of writing this part of my book, February 25th, 2020 (my birthday), the Coronavirus has been declared a national emergency by "WHO" (World Health Organization), not yet a pandemic but close. It has been declared an epidemic by many countries. Tens of thousands have died in China. Thousands have been stranded in foreign countries, or they have been unable to leave cruise ships as traveling to and from Asia has come to a virtual standstill through quarantining precautions. It has made its way to Italy and North America, already with deaths.

"Coronavirus", the meaning taken from WHO is: "(CoV) are a large family of viruses that cause illness ranging from the common cold to more severe diseases such as Middle East Respiratory Syndrome (MERS-CoV) and Severe Acute Respiratory Syndrome (SARS-CoV). The "novel-coronavirus" (nCOViD-19) is a new strain that has not been previously identified in humans." Further, "coronaviruses are zoonotic, meaning they are transmitted between animals and people." Detailed investigation found that SARS-CoV was transmitted from civet (small, lean nocturnal native to tropical Asia and Africa) cats to humans.

The common cold was the first, most simplistic definition of a coronavirus. We still cannot cure, or prevent the common cold.

And, while many will use the argument that today's strain is previously undetected, if we had learned to cure the cold a long time ago, these strains might very well have never evolved.

Meanwhile, we've supposedly landed on the moon trying to reach the heavens.

We've built the Hadron Particle Collider in Geneva Switzerland that smashes atoms in hopes of finding the "missing link, the Higgs-Bosun-The God-Particle" — all part of particle physics theory. "Theory!" Millions if not billions were spent on creating this, based on "theory!"

We've learned how to clone an animal! That means we've learned to believe we can play God. God, whoever you believe in, was the only one who could create a living being. That has been sacred. But we human beings, and our quest for doing the impossible and seeing ourselves as the superior being, have gotten in our own way.

We can now transmit a message to the other side of the world in a millisecond via the Internet. We can send videos and the complete text of a book via Facebook in same time. We can stay home and look for potential relationships via dating sites without physically interacting with each other.

Star Trek and its virtual reality was created not too long ago where we put on a headset and see ourselves in a make-believe setting — even taking part. And now the next level is called Augmented Reality (AR), again from *Star Trek* and its holographic imagery (three dimensional (3D) phantom images hovering is real space), where we can try on products like sunglasses, how a gun looks on our hands or, slip our foot into a 3D ghost image of the exact shoe we are interested in so we can see how it looks and how it fits before buying in "on-line" (over the Internet) — all while we are sitting in the comfort of our home sipping on a glass of wine or beer.

As stated in the beginning of this book, Mechatronics is the future, but it is also very much the "now."

Robotics and automation having been part of manufacturing

is not new. The next step, however, leads to artificial intelligence, which will continue to grow by leaps and bounds. Predictions of job losses due to robotics taking over more and more human labour tasks are very much real. It is the reality of today, in fact! It is happening now!

Is that a good thing, or a bad thing? Is it positive evolution of the inevitable? Yes, it gives us more time for ourselves, but where does our income come from then? Can it lead to a stagnant society; a lazy lifestyle where we don't feel compelled to work hard to earn a living?

Kid yourself not. The fears that Detective Spooner played by Will Smith in the movie, *I, Robot*, based on Isaac Asimov's book of the same title, are getting closer and closer ...

"Robots building robots? Now that's just stupid."
Detective Spooner

But, we still cannot cure or prevent the common cold.

The speed of life today brings a great deal of excitement for the future. It brings hope of an easier life in every way imaginable. It does bring hope of better health, but remember, like any thing involving money, there is politics and, of course, manipulation based on greed. Again I say, if you repeat something enough times, with charisma and power in your voice, the people who struggle to think freely for themselves will suffer from physiological scotoma and start believing it because they feel they should; the shepherd leading the sheep — still!

We are far too busy comparing with what we don't have — trying to be first, the best, living with a MeFirst mindset, and trying to achieve higher and higher levels so we can feel power. It's the wrong type of power. Ironically it takes the right type of power (focus) in order to achieve that level of "hurtful" and "controlling" power. That's when we lose control of our mind. That's when the feeling of "wanting more, wanting it all" appears and takes us over and we become someone else based on outside influence and manipulation.

Once again, please don't get me wrong. It's a great feeling to win, to be the best at what you do after all the hard work you put into excelling. When you lose your soul, your sense of "self," is when it's gone too far and you are no longer a free thinker.

Chapter 11

Social Media Meltdown

"Whoever controls the media, controls the mind"
   Baaaaaaa…..Jim Morrison

And then there's the influence of media as seen by the late, great musician and philosopher, Jim Morrison of *The Doors*.

This is "your" mind he is talking about! Are you okay with being controlled? This very thing is happening today more than ever before.

I want to relive my glory years — my teenage and young adult years — but with the knowledge and tools of today's young generation's skills with social media. But please, please grab me and put me in isolation for a week to start, if you find me standing at the edge of a street as killer vehicles go whizzing past me less than a metre away, all while I have my head down and eyes transfixed on my cell phone.
No, check that, even if I'm just walking down the sidewalk. Wait, I'll go even further — if I take my cell phone into school with me and allow my mind to go soft while I use its calculator to do simple multiplication and divisional mathematics; and of course this is all in between while I'm trying to focus on checking Facebook or Tinder messages during the annoying and very distracting lesson my teacher is giving us students.
Definitely then, please put me away and let me think about it for a while. Let me think about my connection and even more

importantly my awareness, my consciousness of my surroundings.

People have a voice, which can, in an instant, become the powerful collective, and wow, do we use/abuse it on social media! "Interactive software" includes: MSN Hotmail as being one of the first with Microsoft Outlook leading to Instant Messaging with MSN Messenger which led to IRC (Internet Relay Chat, a multi-user system allowing people to gather on "channels" or "rooms" to talk "privately").

Privately? Once people realised how this all works, the imagination took it to what seems to be limitless possibilities. Still — and with anything there is both pros and cons — Facebook became the people's choice, at least for a good long time. It was also the choice of those who wanted to manipulate and influence. For the older generations, to use Facebook made one feel smart and with the times. It also made one much more gullible.

Social media can be so much fun, but it is the new marketing tool for the masses. The ease of how messages can be repeated over and over again, even with subtle changes that the psychologists have determined will "hook" the viewer's mind, shows the new level of influence people are subjected to.

It's time to quote an earlier question I asked in The Living Order, regarding the use of social media:

"Is it your ability to voice your opinion on social media — enough to get attention where one's possible malevolent nature tries to influence the narrative with nasty and vulgar comments regarding what others post? One's low self-esteem has found a faceless avenue of attack for the sad zealot. Is it how well you score on dating sites?"

Social media is the armchair quarterback's, the bully's, and the narcissist's best friend. It is a gift to those needy of self-gratification where they can gather attention and influence without much accountability. It has become a forum for those

Human Mechatronics™: The Double-Edged Power of Influence

who need to vent and rant when they can't handle rejection. They take it out on someone or some company and try their best to ruin their reputation. That is all about how weak and needy they are. To those reading that behave this very way - do you accept that about yourself? Why? No matter what your past is, you can learn to live. Everyone else, other than your own archetype cronies sees this behaviour as your weakness - it is who you have let yourself become - not who you were meant to be. Add a live news network to it, and you get people walking in behind, or even in front of, a live broadcast, while they hold their cell phone up so that can get in the picture and post it on Facebook. The need for attention and to feel important is so contrived and artificial through these acts.

Social media can be cruel — hatefully cruel. There are good people in this world and there are bad people. Like a driver behind the wheel of a motor vehicle — social media is where the worst in people can appear with maximum darkness and where bullies in groups can gang up together and tear good souls apart.

In the list mentioned in Chapter 9 was Mercedes Grabowski, known as August Ames. I have never heard about her until writing and researching for this book. For some reason known only to her, she chose to be a pornographic movie actress and model, and became a star.

What I do know is that many who turn to the pornographic industry choose it as a way out when they don't feel they have other options that will pay nearly as well. The trade-off to the money is selling one's soul to the control and greed, and abuse, of those that own the adult entertainment industry. They may not see it as such, living through it, but in the end, from what I've learned, the soul eventually re-appears seeking absolution.

Make no mistake about it; it's almost a mob-mentality within management of the industry. The money is ridiculously rampant because watching porn movies is at an all-time high. Supply and demand rules.

August Ames' mother suffered from bipolar disorder. Ames alleges that, as a child, her paternal grandfather routinely sexually assaulted her, but that her father refused to believe her.

She was sent to a group home, and then became a nanny, animal-assistant aide, and horseback trainer.

Once in the porn industry she made over 290 films and was nominated for an AVN (Adult Video News) Award, ironically for non-pornographic films.

She made the decision to say "no" to performing in a certain type of porn movie. Ames died by suicide after a certain event created social media backlash following a Twitter post that she had made. It destroyed her for doing the right thing.

August had been caught in a firestorm of a different kind. After tweeting that she would "not" act with a "cross-over" co-star who had filmed gay scenes, the wrath of the porn industry and Twitter at large descended upon her.

There was gay porn star Jaxton Wheeler who said August should take a cyanide pill. Then veteran actress Jessica Drake whose more oblique tweets were framed as cyberbullying, and then finally August's husband, porn producer Kevin Moore lashed out at her.

It became too much. Out of principle she was acting for herself — for her own integrity — and believe you me, there is much integrity even in the adult entertainment/porn industry, but as mentioned before, once in it, you have sold your soul and God be with you. You feel trapped. Mercedes was trapped within August, who was trapped by the greed and power of the industry, which in turn was fed by the public. When she took her own life, she was only 23 years of age.

August is the subject of an audio book, *The Last Days of August*. It's an investigation by journalist Jon Ronson and producer Lina Misitzis. (Source: Wikipedia)

Human Mechatronics™: The Double-Edged Power of Influence

This is one case. Each case in chapter 9 is fascinating, and very sad. It's very sad because once again, so many, at a young age, have dealt with childhood pressures that evolved from childhood joys. How does a child rationally deal with pressure? They don't! The fact that they are so trusting and impressionable at a young age, as they should be for positive growth, is so often taken advantage of and led astray to the dark side, involving great money and material things. Their environment and upbringing becomes them.

The world today is full of distractions, many of which come with negative energy. Today more than ever before, with television and video games being controlled by money and power, when social media is so much part of most people's lives, it is hard to focus on the positive. Whether it's in politics, mental heath struggles, abuse of power, runaways, human trafficking, poverty, immigration, bullying, suicide becoming epidemic, scandals involving our idols and our heroes, people we trust lying so much no one knows the truth anymore, interference from outside countries, narcissism, sales and marketing — we are being hit left-right-top-centre with outside influence.

These are fun things to do though, right? Playing video games is a blast. Long gone are the games of *Pong*, *Pac Man* and *Galaxia*. *The Game of Thrones* rules these days.

From the 2008 movie *Fool's Gold* with Kate Hudson as Tess and Matthew McConaughey as Finn when they are trying to stay alive in an airplane:
Tess: "Where'd you learn to fly?"
Finn: "You know, Playstation!"

Social media and video games have caused a severe meltdown of human principles, morals, sensitivity and respect. The influence we get through the games, the Internet and especially social media is highly intelligent yet highly manipulative; so much so that we often don't know the difference between what's fact and what's fiction.

We also need regular news media — radio, television, live news, etc... Sadly, it is also inundated with drama to create higher rating reviews and thus, more money. Social media is all about advertising and money — don't let anyone tell you different. We need the news though! We need to be informed, otherwise it is left to people of power to influence and manipulate us, the public, into thinking and believing in what they want us to believe. Scotoma!

With regular news and in particular with its "real-time" broadcasting, the "live" image shown on a video is fact. What you see is what it is. It is, and what you heard, is fact! The narrative, however, can bend the desired perception. Welcome to the new age of propaganda. It's always been a challenge to know what to believe. Conspiracy theories and mistrust have always been there, and advocated by those in search of power. Today, the influence has become international as another way of creating a cold war. It is not all fake, and not any one station is fake in it of themselves. Much of it, however, does come with a bias leaning to one side or the other of an angle of persuasion.

And then there is the political arena. In this day and age, with American President Trump using Twitter to connect with the world, I would feel irresponsible if I did not address this. I promise to do my best to stay impartial and neutral to any side taken. I do, however, read news articles that I like to share.

In a CNN news article dated May 28, 2020, with the headline, "Trump is set to announce an executive order against social media companies", Jason Miller, the communications director for Trump's 2016 campaign and someone who has been directly involved with Trump's social media strategy, cleverly praised Mr. Trump for his ability to connect with and influence the people. "It is one of President Trump's super powers," Miller said. "He understood very early on that social media, Twitter in particular, gave him unvarnished access to the American people and his supporters. What Trump maximized was social media's ability to bypass the artificial conversation created by the mainstream media." It is true, Mr. Trump is a master at knowing how to manipulate the people and embrace them as his sheep.

Not everything is bad about news media and social media. I enjoy both. Social media helps me stay connected with friends: past, present, work, living order groups, world order groups, and it's amazing to see what all are doing even though you are reading something they wrote up to make themselves look good and maybe myself included ;-)

It can become very addictive and even hypnotizing. And that is what we have to remember. The professional manipulators are ahead of the firewalls and anti-virus software we use. They prey on human desires. They prey on human, and especially youth's, adventurous and visual desire of sex. They prey on teasing the hormones and need to "look good" and "feel good" personal quest. We either run towards the influence wanting it desperately, or we run away — hating how it makes us feel lousy — lowering one's self-esteem in comparison.

And most of all, they prey on reaching the public at as young an age as possible; molding a child who does not have the wisdom for rationalizing, for being intuitive, for being experienced about deciding who to trust and who not to trust vs. recognizing the "fight or flight" feeling and walking away. Control of this young age is very easy for the adult influencer to achieve.

Youth are introduced to social media at far too early and freely of a young age these days, and with full trust of parents to believe they will be able to figure it out for themselves. But then people shout out, "It's my right!"

For an eight-year-old, one graphic image, one image of a young female, totally naked, lying strategically yet seductively on a couch, leaving everything to one's imagination — or, one video of pornographic material, which is so easy to find, can influence them for the rest of their life. And sadly they won't realize its damaging effects until they get older, if they even do ever realize it.

But, we still cannot cure or prevent the common cold.

Chapter 9

Are You Trapped?

All I have tried to do with everything you have read so far is to help you think for yourself, understand more how you became what you are today, and open up your mind.

Take this book once again, go stand in front of a mirror, look at yourself and now ask the following questions once more:

1st question: Who am I?

Is it tougher now? Remember to have fun. Pause if you wish, then answer the question. Now answer it again out loud.

2nd question: What influences helped make me who I am?

Pause if you wish, then answer the question. Now answer it again out loud.

3rd question: Did I decide, of my own free will, to be who I am today?

Pause if you wish, then answer the question. Now answer it again out loud.

4th question (bonus): Am I honestly happy with who — and where I am today?

Pause if you wish, then answer the question. Now answer it again out loud.

Many people, being 100% honest with themselves, will answer #4 question with, "Yes. I am!"

Great! Good for you! I am happy for you. Keep Rock'in!!

Yet, many people, also being 100% honest with themselves, will answer #4 question with, "No. I am not!" Great! Good for you! I am happy for you in that you have just shown the incredible strength to admit that truth! Doing so, admitting one is not happy, or that they are depressed, or that they have made mistakes, is NOT a weakness. THAT IS STRENGTH!! Feel proud.

If you don't answer honestly, then be prepared to feel trapped! Far too many people are trapped in their own world, in their own being, in their own mind where their past, and present, constantly falls victim to triggers which prevent the enjoyment of a real life based on one's own free thinking.

It is also so easy, when we struggle with focus, to get caught up in the world, the life around us today that feeds us energy, whether positive or negative — we are being bombarded by it and absorb it into our subconscious mind. Remember from the beginning of this book, the definition of a Look v.s. a Glance. If you look at the negative influence, at the distractions, you will become them. A Glance is no more than 1-second. Say it out loud, "One-thousand one." That's it! Then look where YOU want to go.

Your Human Machine is the most incredible machine ever built! Regardless of how you feel right this moment, do not ever forget that! You may feel great. You may feel miserable. You may feel successful. You may feel like a failure. You may feel alive and wanted. You may feel alone and invisible. Right now, right this moment, I am going to tell you that it is okay! Right this moment you are successful, you rock and I am proud of you! Why? Because you are reading this and that means you have made it to this point! You have survived whatever you have lived through and you are still alive and breathing.

All of the above feelings are just that — feelings. Feelings can and will change. You "will" take control of your own mind and think for yourself. In order to do that, you may need to ask for help. It is a monumental show of your strength when you ask for help. Yes, some people, from the dark side, will chastise you and make fun. They will "try" their best at making you feel badly about yourself. There will unfortunately always be "Haters" — the disgruntled, the naysayers who claim that everything that is not to their belief, is fake. Remember, they are the bullies and it's because they feel badly about themselves, they don't like themselves. It's not about you!

Negative energy, like fast foods tasting so good, lures us in because we are craving for some "good feeling vibration." We have the ability ourselves to create that good feeling vibration!

There is so much good, even great in this world of ours! Everything that has been discussed here in this book has a double-edge to it. There is good and bad in: faith, religion, politics, group behaviour, individual behaviour, stardom and fame, and in us, the people. We need, and most of us want, all the above. The power of Influence however, can be so strong, that you can lose who you really are as freethinkers for ourselves. We want to matter, but we must matter first of all to our own "self." How do you want to be remembered when and after you die?

I hope this book has opened up your mind to the how and why people, cultures, societies, and nations behave the way they do: be it good or bad behavior. That was the intent – to review how we can be manipulated and influenced without sometimes even being aware of it happening.

From the 1969 song, One Tin Soldier, written by Dennis Lambert and Brian Potter and first performed by Canadian band, The Original Caste, then became the theme song performed by Coven, in the avant-garde-Hollywood changing 1971 pro-racial, social and indigenous justice indie-action movie, Billy Jack, written by and co-starring husband-wife team Tom Laughlin and Delores Taylor (Source: Wikipedia and www.billyjack.com),

Craig Dubecki

"Now they stood beside the treasure,
On the mountain dark and red.
Turned the stone and looked beneath it,
Peace on Earth was all it said."

Looking forward, let us now learn what we can do about all this and gain that "true focus" and "true power" in order to constructively live the way we want, and deserve to!

Welcome to the world of Human Mechatronics™, DotsDoConnect™, Quadratic Cognition™, and The WYLIWYG® Principle coming out later in 2020 in Book 2: Human Mechatronics: The Power of Focus Introducing The WYLIWYG® Principle

Part 2: Human Mechatronics™: The Power Behind Your "Self"
Focus: A Look vs. A Glance
The Human Machine
The Brain: Wired vs. Programmed
The Mind: The CPU That Is You!
Aptitude: Now It's Up To You
Why You Are You: Good or Bad
Quadrantic Cognition™: Maximum Focus: The Zone
Distractions: Intentional and Unintentional
The Underappreciated E.T.

Part 3: DotsDoConnect™
Focus: A Look vs. A Glance
Dots vs. Holes: Success vs. Failure
Embracing Your Past
Daddy, Mommy
Teach Your Parents Well
Disconnecting To Reconnect

Part 4: The WYLIWYG® Principle
Focus: A Look vs. A Glance
Child's Play: Aptitude
You Are A Free Thinker with Discipline
Your World Today
Finding a Drive in Life to Drive Your Life™
WYLIWYG: Where You Look Is Where You Go®

About the Author

CRAIG DUBECKI is an active volunteer with numerous associations in the Kitchener-Waterloo region of Ontario, Canada, in particular with Suicide Prevention and Heart & Stroke. Along with being a Marketing Manager with multi-trade industrial contractor, he is a:

- Published author
- Performing musician
- Accomplished and recognized Toastmaster speaker, evaluator and judge with the Diversecity chapter in Kitchener, Ontario, Canada
- Public speaker with the Professional Speaker Associations (PSA) and Momondays
- Member of Adlerian Society

Craig is a cognitive authority and life coach, using non-complex analogies and human experiences to entertain and help people be the best they can and rock their life. Craig created and is owner of:

The WYLIWYG® Principle: WYLIWYG (pronounced: Will-eee-wig): Where You Look Is Where You Go®, a Principle designed to help the audience find the personal power of true focus.

Human Mechatronics™
Quadrantic Cognition™
DotsDoConnect™

Books written or co-authored by Craig Dubecki and all found on Craig's website, www.DotsDoConnect.com

#1: *So, You Just Want To Be A RockStar*, 2015 (also found on Amazon).
A musically driven, psychological adventure through life based on what we all, when we are young, want to find - how to be a Rockstar in our own world. This is also the first book of a trilogy later carried on with the following noted, Sharing Volume 4 and, Dreaming BIG Being BOLD Volume 3.

#2: *The Encore: Roll With The Changes*, the 2nd part of the Trilogy in his first anthology, *Sharing: our stories, our selves, our successes, Volume 4, an anthology of men's empowerment stories, 2017,* created by Lisa Browning, *One Thousand Trees*.

#3: *What Are You Looking At?* in the Best Selling anthology, *Dreaming BIG Being BOLD Volume 3, Inspiring Stories from Trailblazers, Visionaries and Change Makers, 2017, Craig's second anthology* created by Paula Morand and Victoria Craig, and final story of his trilogy.

#4: *Human Mechatronics: The Double-Edged Power of Influence*, 2020.

"To live in darkness and pain is sometimes more than one person can handle. That's when we need to reach out and ask for help. That is strength! Let's make life the adventure it was meant to be! What are you looking at?" Craig Dubecki

www.DotsDoConnect.com

Suggested Further Readings
(other than the previous books I've written)

1. *The Fire Next Time* by James Baldwin
2. *The Warmth of Other Suns* by Isabel Wilkerson
3. *Their Eyes Were Watching God* by Zora Neale Hurston
4. *So You Want To Talk About Race* by Ijeoma Oluo
5. *Eloquent Rage: A Black Feminist Discovers Her Superpower* by Dr. Brittany Cooper
6. *I'm Still Here: Black Dignity In a World Made For Whiteness* by Austin Channing Brown
7. *The Bluest Eye* by Toni Morrison
8. *Policing Black Lives* by Robyn Maynard
9. *The Shack* by William P. Young
10. *The Piñata Theory: What's in Your Stuffing?* by Charlene Renaud
11. *The Celestine Prophecy* by James Redfield
12. *The Seven Habits of Highly Effective People* by Stephen Covey
13. *Think and Grow Rich* by Napoleon Hill
14. *What Life Could Mean To You* by Alfred Adler
15. *Wisdom for Life, it's Child's Play* by Michael Moore
16. *Through My Eyes* by Ruby Bridges
17. *Ruby Bridges Goes To School: My True Story* by Ruby Bridges